WOULD-BE WIFE KILLER

WOULD-BE WIFE KILLER

A Clinical Study of
Primitive Mental Functions,
Actualised Unconscious
Fantasies,
Satellite States, and
Developmental Steps

Vamık D. Volkan

KARNAC

First published in 2015 by
Karnac Books Ltd
118 Finchley Road
London NW3 5HT

British Library Cataloguing in Publication Data

A C.I.P. for this book is available from the British Library

ISBN-13: 978-1-78220-279-0

Typeset by V Publishing Solutions Pvt Ltd., Chennai, India

Printed and bound in Great Britain by TJ International Ltd, Padstow

www.karnacbooks.com

CONTENTS

ABOUT THE AUTHOR

Vamık D. Volkan, M.D., is an emeritus professor of psychiatry at the University of Virginia School of Medicine, Charlottesville, Virginia; an emeritus training and supervising psychoanalyst at the Washington Psychoanalytic Institute, Washington, D.C.; and the Senior Erik Erikson Scholar at the Erikson Institute for Education and Research of the Austen Riggs Center in Stockbridge, Massachusetts. He served as the Medical Director of the University of Virginia's Blue Ridge Hospital and the director of the University of Virginia's Center for the Study of Mind and Human Interaction. He is a past president of the International Society of Political Psychology, the Virginia Psychoanalytic Society, the Turkish-American Neuropsychiatric Association, and the American College of Psychoanalysts. He holds Honorary Doctorate degrees from Kuopio University, Finland (now called University of Eastern Finland); from Ankara University, Turkey; and from Eastern Psychoanalytical University, St. Petersburg, Russia. He served as a member of the Carter Center's International Negotiation Network, headed by former president Jimmy Carter. He was an Inaugural Yitzak Rabin Fellow, Rabin Center for Israeli Studies, Tel Aviv, Israel; a Visiting Professor of Law, Harvard University, Boston, Massachusetts; a Visiting Professor of Political Science, the University of Vienna, Vienna, Austria and Bahçeşehir University, Istanbul, Turkey; and a Visiting Professor of Psychiatry, Ankara University, Ankara, Ege University, Izmir and Cerrahpaşa Medical Faculty, Istanbul, Turkey. He chaired the Select Advisory Commission to the Federal Bureau of Investigation's 1996 Critical Incident Response Group; was a Temporary Consultant to the World Health Organization in Albania and Macedonia; and a Fulbright Scholar in Austria. Dr. Volkan received the Nevitt Sanford Award from the International Society of Political Psychology, the Max Hayman Award from the American Orthopsychiatric Association, the L. Bryce Boyer Award from the Society for Psychological Anthropology, the Margaret Mahler Literature Prize from the Margaret Mahler Foundation, Best Teaching Award from the American College of Psychoanalysts, and the Sigmund Freud Award given by the city of Vienna in collaboration with the World Council of Psychotherapy. He has been nominated four times for the Nobel Peace Prize in the mid-2000s and in 2014 with letters of support from twenty-seven countries for examining conflicts between opposing large groups, carrying out projects in various troubled spots in the world for thirty years, and developing psychopolitical theories. At present he is the president of International Dialogue Initiative, a non-profit organisation that brings together unofficial representatives from various parts of the world, including Germany, Iran, Israel, Russia, Turkey, United Kingdom, United States, and West Bank to examine world affairs from a psychopolitical angle. He is the author, co-author, editor, or co-editor of dozens of books, and has served on the editorial boards of sixteen national or international professional journals. He lectures internationally.

ABOUT THIS BOOK

This book tells the story of a man who became my patient soon after I began my psychiatric residency training over five and a half decades ago. The evening before I met him for the first time he had attempted to chop off his wife's head with an axe, but stopped himself from becoming a murderer by entering a catatonic state. He was then a thirty-nine-year-old Methodist minister and I was fourteen years his junior. For nearly five years I saw him every workday during his first three-month-long hospitalisation, during a second hospitalisation of over a month's duration, and then once a week as an outpatient. Following this treatment period I moved to a new location nearly 300 miles away from him, but since I believed that he needed further psychotherapy, I gave him the name of a psychiatrist who had an office not far away from where he lived. He refused to see my colleague, however, and instead drove to my new place and continued to see me once a month for some years. Gradually, he came less frequently—four to six times a year for a decade or so and then once or twice a year—until his physical health started to decline when he was in his mid-seventies. Although I did not see him after this, we spoke on the phone several times before he died in his early eighties. By giving details of my understanding of the mind of this Methodist Minister, I will illustrate the appearance of some primitive mental functions in the daily behaviour of a person who almost became a murderer.

Psychoanalysts have written psychobiographies of historical figures such as Adolph Hitler (Langer, 1972; Dorpat, 2002), who caused unimaginable human tragedy, including mass murder. In the United States, especially after 11 September 2001, there was psychoanalytic interest in examining what makes a person a terrorist, home-grown or otherwise (Volkan, 1997, 2013; Olsson, 2014). The appearance and psychology of murderers and attempted murderers within routine societal conditions, with some exceptions (Duncan, 2002; Fonagy, 2001; Stone, 1989, 2009), have not been studied in depth by psychoanalysts. One obvious reason for this is that persons who commit homicide, or who are serial or spree killers, or attempted murderers do not come for psychoanalytic treatment and do not spend years on a psychoanalyst's couch. Peter Fonagy's paper that describes in great detail the inner world of a killer and her years-long psychoanalytic treatment is most unusual. His patient Henrietta, a young woman, had killed her boyfriend by stabbing him during a violent quarrel (Fonagy, 2001; Fonagy & Target, 2002).

After twenty-year-old Adam Lanza shot and killed his mother and then went directly to Sandy Hook Elementary School in Newton, Connecticut on 14 December 2012, I could not stop thinking about why a person would commit mass murder. This event led me to write *Animal Killer: Transmission of War Trauma from One Generation to the Next* (Volkan, 2014b) to examine the role that certain humiliating childhood events combined with transgenerational transmission of trauma played in turning a man whom I named Peter into a mass killer of animals. Peter would fly in a helicopter over a herd of deer, machinegun the animals, and watch their bellies explode. Peter also killed not only enemy combatants, but also women and children during the Vietnam War. When Peter was a very small child his biological father abandoned him, and a man who would become his stepfather entered his life and "saved" him from a smothering, humiliating home environment. Peter's stepfather was a survivor of the 1942 Bataan Death March and Japanese war camps in the Philippines. He deposited his self-representation, severely traumatised during World War II, into the developing self-representation of little Peter and tasked him with being a vicious hunter instead of one who is hunted. Peter had a prestigious job in the American weapons industry and friends who were high-level politicians. But when he faced a humiliating event, such as perceived rejection by his wife or disappointment due to a work situation, he needed to kill animals.

Common to both Peter and the potential wife killer I describe in this book are experiences of shame, humiliation, repeated helpless rage, and consequent aggression in their struggles to achieve psychological separation from the mental representations of their smothering mothers, in Peter's case also a grandmother. Even so, their personality organisations were different: Peter had a malignant narcissistic personality organisation and the Methodist minister had a psychotic one. Peter's motivation to be an animal killer was quite specific and unique to him, with no similarity to the Methodist minister's motivation to cut off his wife's head. We can say that each murderer's, or potential murderer's, psychodynamic processes need to be understood on individual bases.

The most effective way to learn and/or teach psychodynamic concepts, including those that may explain extreme sadism and deadly violence in a person, is to illustrate their appearance in clinical work, especially when experienced psychoanalysts describe them through relating a patient's treatment from its beginning to its termination. After I became a psychoanalyst in the early 1970s, owing to my administrative and teaching duties and my involvement in psychopolitical projects in different parts of the world (Volkan, 1988, 1997, 2004a, 2006, 2013, 2014a), I devoted what limited time I had for clinical practice primarily to conducting psychoanalysis. I seldom saw patients less than four times a week in psychotherapy. Throughout the decades I have written *total* psychoanalytic processes of several of my analysands who had different personality organisations, in order to illustrate how detailed clinical observations are needed to explain theoretical concepts clearly (Volkan, 1973, 1974, 1987, 1995, 2010; Volkan & Ast, 1997; Volkan & Fowler, 2009). Even though the potential wife killer I describe in this book was one of my psychotherapy cases and was not on my couch, I follow the same tradition here and detail stories of my work with this patient over four decades starting from the first day I met him. The content of this book, besides illustrating why one individual almost became a murderer, includes:

- Description of the psychology of severe physical injury in childhood on a boy's body part that stands for a penis
- Observation of the appearance of "*actualised* unconscious fantasies" due to such an injury, and the utilisation of such a fantasy in

adapting to life and developing a variety of symptoms, including hallucinations and delusions

- Presentation of a conceptual system that emphasises psychic structure (personality organisation) that expands our evaluation of intrapsychic conflicts in understanding psychopathology
- Visualisation of the image of a jelly-filled doughnut to define a "psychotic core" and explore its fate
- Investigation of primitive transference and countertransference manifestations that primarily exhibit themselves through fusion-diffusion or internalisation–externalisation processes of various self- and object images accompanied by introjective-projective cycles of affects and thoughts
- Illustration of how patients with a psychotic core tolerate "emotional flooding", how they begin to utilise anxiety as a signal of a psychological conflict, and how they accomplish identification with the therapist as "a new object" while developing new and more adaptive ego functions
- Definition of how patients with psychotic-level personality organisation begin to comprehend a "symbol" and how they change their internal psychological structure and develop more ability to test reality
- Evaluation of "linking interpretations" and "therapeutic plays" in which patients repeat in action the story of an unconscious fantasy but, with therapeutic help, finish it in a more adaptive way, illustrating their new and more adaptive ego functions
- Conceptualisation of "satellite state" in which individuals find a balance between experiencing individuation and remaining dependent on the Other, like a small child who can enjoy playing in a room alone or with other children as long as she can, now and then, rush to the kitchen and briefly touch her mother
- Description of "crucial juncture" experiences: an adult patient learning to integrate his self- and object images
- Realisation of how traumas caused by severe surgeries can open up previously healed psychological wounds
- Attention to cultural and religious differences in the backgrounds of two persons, the patient and the therapist, working intimately together for a long time.

In this book I also hope to illustrate my nostalgia for times when many clinicians worked hard to understand the inner lives of very severely disturbed persons and tried to make them more functional instead of, as is unfortunately too often the case now, simply medicating them into submission, even sometimes "throwing" many of them out in the streets.

While this book primarily focuses on my relationship with one individual, the Methodist minister, stories of other persons in treatment are also presented in order to better illustrate certain theoretical and technical concepts.

Decades after his attempt to kill his wife, the subject of this book became a beloved leader of his community. His case is most fascinating. Since I knew him over many decades, he was part of my life. I am dedicating this book to his memory.

CHAPTER ONE

A beginning therapist meets a would-be wife murderer

I was born to Turkish parents in Cyprus, a Mediterranean island located south of Turkey. I left the island for the first time in 1950 when I was eighteen years old and went to Turkey to study medicine at Ankara University. I graduated in June 1956 and in early February 1957 I came to the United States with only fifteen dollars in my pocket and my violin under my arm. In Ankara, besides attending medical school, I was a member of an amateur orchestra that performed concerts now and then. Before leaving Turkey I had secured an internship position at the Lutheran Deaconess Hospital in Chicago, where I began working as soon as I arrived. I was part of what was nicknamed the "brain drain" in the 1950s, when many young physicians from foreign countries were lured to the United States to compensate for the shortage of medical professionals there.

The evening after my arrival in Chicago, without any orientation and without even knowing the American names of basic medicines, even simple pain killers, I found myself on-call to respond in my broken English to emergencies for about 600 inpatients. Orientation to the work at the hospital took place two weeks later. A soft-spoken elderly surgeon kindly collected eight much younger physicians, all newcomers from foreign lands, for an orientation. He began by pointing to a telephone and informing us of the name of the instrument, "telephone", and that it sometimes rings. Upon hearing the sound, he told us, we should lift up the handle and before saying "hello" we should smile. Although some in Turkey and Cyprus may not have been able to afford a telephone, I certainly knew what one was and how to use it, and I felt that our host had treated me and the others—all doctors—as poor, ignorant, uncivilised persons. This was my somewhat bewildering introduction to the United States. However, I still feel grateful to the American nursing personnel who were working at the Lutheran Deaconess Hospital at that time for helping and protecting me until I began adjusting to my new surroundings. Later I would learn that the physical plant of the Lutheran Deaconess Hospital was deteriorating, and by 1968 it would be closed and relocated to the northwest in Park Ridge, Illinois.

In the 1950s, most foreign physicians who wanted to become psychiatrists had a tendency to seek work in state mental hospitals following their internships. There were rumours about the governor of one state bragging that there were thousands more emotionally disturbed patients in one of his state's mental hospitals than there were in the largest state mental hospital in a neighbouring state. These hospitals paid physicians from foreign countries higher salaries than they would have received at university hospitals. I come from a family of teachers. My parents, my sisters, my brothers-in-law, my uncle, and other relatives were at that time teaching at all levels, from elementary schools to a medical school, and I was determined to be a teacher too. To prepare for a position in a medical school, I wanted my training as a psychiatrist to take place at a university hospital. Therefore, I was happy when I learned that I had been accepted as a psychiatry resident at the University of North Carolina's North Carolina Memorial Hospital in Chapel Hill. After spending one year in Chicago, a big city, I went to Chapel Hill, then a village.

My experiences as a psychiatry resident at North Carolina University's Memorial Hospital were very different from those of young physicians in training in psychiatry at university hospitals in the United States today. In the mid-1950s psychoanalytic influence was dominant at university hospitals. Many chairpersons and most senior teachers at such places were psychoanalysts, and North Carolina Memorial Hospital was no different. As trainees, we were intensively taught how to interview a patient, make sense of psychodynamic formulations, notice transference manifestations, and make interpretations. I recall being on-call one evening during my first year of residency when one hospitalised patient complained of a severe headache. I prescribed aspirin. The next morning my supervisor learned about this and was upset about my giving the patient a headache pill without first talking with him and finding out the psychological causes of his headache. Part of our education included conducting therapeutic sessions with a patient while being observed behind a one-way mirror by our supervisors and fellow residents in psychiatry. Sometimes the trainees were asked to conduct sessions with patients without asking a single question. This was done to "force" us to learn how to talk and interact with our patients, instead of "machine gunning" them with questions and receiving only short answers. In those days, psychiatric patients could stay at university hospitals for many months if necessary.

After finishing my residency training I worked at two state mental hospitals in North Carolina: one and a half years at Cherry Hospital in Goldsboro and six months at Dorothea Dix Hospital in Raleigh. I was obliged to do so because the state of North Carolina had paid me an additional small salary during my training to become a psychiatrist if I agreed to work at state hospitals for two years after completing my residency training. There were thousands of inpatients in each state hospital with various social and economic backgrounds. My interactions with them and their family members taught me in a most direct fashion about American culture, at least as it expressed itself in the American South. Cherry hospital was a segregated one, and it housed only African-Americans with mental problems. Working there for a year and a half informed me a great deal about the incredible racism and race problems in the United States (Volkan, 2009). At that time no one could have imagined that five decades later an African-American, Barack Obama, would be elected president of the United States. Most physicians at the state mental hospitals in North Carolina and neighbouring states in those days were physicians from different countries—Lithuania, Philippines, Greece, Korea, among others. Looking back, another benefit of working at Cherry Hospital and Dorothea Dix Hospital was getting to know colleagues from different cultures and religions around the world. While working at each of these two state hospitals, I returned to Chapel Hill once a week and continued to benefit from more education and supervision.

After spending five years in North Carolina, in 1963 I moved to Charlottesville, Virginia and became a faculty member at the University of Virginia and a physician at the University Hospital, where I stayed until my retirement in 2002. I became a United States citizen in 1968 and also a candidate at the Washington Psychoanalytic Institute in Washington, DC. I travelled about 120 miles between Charlottesville and Washington, DC again and again for some years to undertake my training analysis and education to become a psychoanalyst.

Let me return to my psychiatric residency days at the North Carolina Memorial Hospital. One day, a few months into my psychiatric training, while I was attending a seminar, a secretary gave me a hand-written message from the head nurse of my psychiatric inpatient unit. She wanted me to come to the unit right away. This was very unusual. I found a telephone, called her, and told her that I was attending a seminar. She sounded very anxious and demanded that I join her right away because I was assigned to work with a new patient and that two policemen who had brought him to the hospital needed to talk with me.

The two policemen looked to be in their mid-twenties, as was I. They seemed to be uncomfortable when they told me that they were from a small rural community about an hour from Chapel Hill and that the man they had brought to the hospital had been their own Methodist minister for the last year. They knew him well since they had attended his church on Sundays rather regularly and heard his sermons. One mumbled: "He is the minister who conducted my marriage ceremony seven months ago." I learned that the minister and his wife had no children. Apparently, they were living in the church parsonage, close to the church and to a cemetery. Not far away stood a Southern Baptist church. There were more Southern Baptists in this region than there were Methodists. I sensed that there was competition between the two churches—both white-only congregations—and these two young policemen wanted to "protect" the reputation of their own minister. However, they had no choice but to tell me about the circumstances leading to the patient's admission to the hospital.

After receiving a call in the wee hours of the morning from the minister's wife, the head policeman, a Southern Baptist, and one of the young policemen who was talking to me, rushed to the minister's house. They found the Methodist minister in the family bedroom standing over the bed he had been sharing with his wife, in a "frozen" state, holding an axe above his head as if he were ready to chop something. The door to the backyard was open. His wife told the policemen how, when she and her husband had both gone to bed the evening before, he had been upset because he had conducted too many funeral ceremonies during the previous weeks. He told his wife that he might kill her and also conduct her funeral ceremony. She stated that she had not been alarmed because she had not believed him. Very early that morning she awoke to find her husband in his pyjamas standing over her with an expression of rage on his face, the lifted axe in his hands. After she screamed, her husband said nothing and seemed to "freeze". She quickly got out of bed and called the police. When they arrived, the head policeman took the axe from the hands of the minister who remained in the same position, motionless. Because of this strange state of mind, instead of taking him to the police station or jail, they called a local physician to come and evaluate him. Prior to bringing him to Chapel Hill, the two young policemen had changed the Methodist minister's clothes from pyjamas to dress clothes, complete with a bow tie, to make him more presentable.

At one point I noticed one of the policemen turn to the other, the newlywed, and whisper, "I used to think that the Baptist pastor was spreading a rumour that our minister was crazy. But, you know, our minister *is* crazy. Remember my telling you two weeks ago about my seeing him in the cemetery next to the church. I swear that he was talking to dead people! The Baptist guy's rumour is true. Our minister talks to ghosts! Our congregation tries to hide it just so the Baptist pastor, that son of a devil, won't be pleased."

The two policemen gave me a two-page handwritten note from the local physician who had "committed" the patient to the university psychiatric unit, authorising the policemen to take him to Chapel Hill. The note said that the patient was thirty-nine years old, and a brief medical examination showed that he was in good physical condition. The physician was aware that the Methodist minister had previously had some "mental problems". Apparently, authorities of the Methodist Church had been routinely assigning him to small rural churches. The physician's diagnosis of the patient's condition was "acute catatonic schizophrenia", and the physician had given him a strong sedative prior to his transportation to North Carolina Memorial Hospital.

Soon after the policemen left, the minister's wife arrived at the hospital and I joined Rebecca, an experienced social worker much older than me, to hear what the woman had to say. Gloria was a beautiful, well-dressed woman with a smile on her face. She did not seem to be frightened or in a panic state. She told us that she was an elementary school teacher and school administrator in the town where she and her husband lived. We learned that she was a few years younger than her husband and they had been married for twelve years. She described how her husband had had on and off "psychiatric problems". Several times he had been given leaves of absence from work, been hospitalised, and had received medications, each time returning to his duties as a Methodist minister. After being away from work, he would often be reassigned to a new church, always in a rural area. In fact, since their marriage they had moved to a new location every three years or so. Gloria was grateful to the Methodist Church authorities for protecting her husband.

Gloria told us that the patient's father had died from a heart condition when the patient was twenty-two years old, five years before they married. His mother had died a year ago when he was thirty-eight years old. Apparently his mother's death had made him very anxious. His wife believed that her husband was not able to grieve and mourn his mother's death in the usual way. Sometimes he called his wife by his dead mother's name. She had the impression that, as the first anniversary of the mother's death approached, he had become preoccupied with the cemetery next to the church. He would tell his wife that his mother and his father might come to their house from the cemetery. In reality, his parents were not buried there. Gloria admitted that her husband had informed her of his plan to cut her throat when they were getting ready for bed, hours before he actually went out, fetched an axe, and then "froze" standing next to their bed. She imparted all this information without exhibiting emotion, as if she were reading news from a newspaper.

Rebecca and I thought that Gloria was in shock from this life-threatening experience. We also thought that as a "good wife" of a Methodist minister she did not wish to speak too much about "bad things" and wished to present her husband as harmless. She was willing to remain with him after his discharge from the hospital, and she did not think that he would try to kill her again.

I then went to see the patient. He was a tall, handsome man with blue eyes. With his nice clothes and bow tie he looked as if he was ready to give a sermon or attend a social event. His brown hair was well combed, and I imagined that either one of the policemen or Gloria had combed it before he was taken to Chapel Hill. He sat on a chair in his hospital room with a forced smile on his face. After I introduced myself he spoke to me, saying things such as, "God blesses us all," and "Today is sunny and nice." He quoted several passages, apparently from the Bible. He then asked me if I was sent by Pastor Johns to take him to the eternity of hell. I suspected that Pastor Johns was the Baptist minister from his community. The patient insisted that everyone is entitled to God's grace. He made many references to Jesus Christ and informed me that Christ died for all humanity, and that even criminals and African Americans and foreigners were entitled to his love. I am sure he had noticed that I was foreign, but he made no reference to my accent.

When I was growing up, Cyprus—populated by Greeks, Turks, and small minorities such as Armenians and Phoenicians—was a British colony. The Greeks are Christians and the Turks are Muslims. During my childhood and teenage years, in most areas of the island they lived next to one another. My parents were under the influence of the first Turkish President Kemal Atatürk's modernisation efforts in the new Turkish Republic, which was established in 1923 after World War I ended and after the Ottoman Empire collapsed. Because, as Cypriot Turks, they lived outside of mainland Turkey and longed for their "motherland", I believe that my parents, like most other Cypriot Turks, invested intensely in Atatürk's cultural revolution. Their exposure to Greek culture and the British administration also played a role in their acceptance and assimilation of Atatürk's modernisation and Westernisation efforts. Many intellectual Cypriot Turks of that time perceived the extreme religious influences in the Ottoman Empire as having kept the Turks from embracing modernisation and as having played a crucial role in the fall of the Ottoman Empire.

Due to my parents' guidance I grew up with very little investment in practising religion. I did not even learn to recite a prayer. As a youngster, when I watched Greeks going to their churches and Turks going to their mosques, I would wonder why people were involved in rituals and beliefs that reflected, in my mind, magical thinking. I was only a cultural Muslim and as a child celebrated Muslim religious days without knowing the reasons they were considered "holy." I was also taught to be respectful towards all religions. During my childhood and teenage years I did not read the Quran and knew little about its stories except the ones I learned from people I met in daily interactions or from books and movies based on religious stories. Therefore, while working with the Methodist minister I had to learn some Bible stories from fellow residents or friends. I would read much of the Bible and the Quran many decades later when I was studying Christian cults and extreme Muslim religious terrorism, because I wanted to know the stories and passages used to support destructive actions (Volkan, 2010; Volkan & Kayatekin, 2006).

In 1958 at North Carolina Memorial Hospital I was facing a man who wanted to cut off his wife's head and who, when we met, constantly mentioned Jesus Christ, God, and quoted passages from the Bible. I felt ignorant about things that he was "throwing" at me and thought that I would not be able to work with him. However, I had never met an individual who actually wanted to cut off his wife's head, and I was very interested in knowing the mind of an attempted murderer.

The next day, when I received supervision from the psychiatrist who was in charge of the inpatient services, I expressed my reservations about working with this patient. My supervisor, who was Jewish, told me that my patient's references to religion, Jesus, and God, might be in the service of his search for an object to stabilise him, an external superego. He added that my patient had not developed an integrated superego and that his uncertainty about finding a harsh versus benign superego was confusing to him.

After listening to my account of some of the patient's statements from the day before, my supervisor added that the patient was most likely comparing Southern Baptist and Methodist belief systems, and was assessing which one was better suited for a needed superego, while wondering if I was a follower of the Baptist pastor, an enemy. I was advised to provide a benign superego model for my patient, sit with him in his room each working day for fifty minutes, tell him that I wanted to get to know him and that whenever he was ready he could share his thoughts and feelings with me. If I noticed that something made the patient very anxious I could share my observation of his condition with the patient, advising him that I was not in a hurry and that he could take his time to let me get to know him. With this approach, I would slowly collect data about his life story. My supervisor also dealt with my anxiety by telling me that he was not in a hurry to hear my formulation about the patient's mental condition. I accepted the case assignment without making any further fuss.

Soon after the patient was admitted to the hospital he was given psychological tests. The experienced psychologist stated that it was difficult to administer psychological tests to the patient because of his inattention. She also admitted that she was afraid of him because she had been told he was a potential murderer. Nevertheless she concluded that he was suffering from "chronic schizophrenia". Later in this book I will return to the diagnosis of the Methodist minister's mental state and examine it closely. In those days there were no sophisticated tools to look at patients' brain functions and so no intensive neurological examination was performed.

During our first meeting I had noticed that the index finger of the patient's right hand was missing. I would learn the story of his missing finger later. He had lost it when he was four years old, and this event turned out to be a most significant event in his life. In the next chapter the reader will learn this story and why, when I wrote about this patient in my first book decades ago (Volkan, 1976), I called him "Attis".

CHAPTER TWO

A man with three penises and two vaginas

The repressing function of Attis' ego was not strong. He would recall events in his early and late childhood in detail and describe them without expressing affects. Once he informed me about seeing his mother's vagina at the age of nine months. Obviously this was a fantasised "memory". On other occasions he described his mother's vagina when he saw it while she was urinating in a field after harvesting vegetables when her son was only three or four years old. Of course, I could not be sure if these recollections were real events or imagined ones. He could also recall certain wishes that most men do not possess or totally repress. For example, in his early teens Attis had wishes and dreams of having sex with his mother even though he considered such acts as frightening. In spite of his interchanging or mixing his fantasies, wishes, and dreads with realities, having delusions and hallucinations that I will illustrate later, and sometimes becoming preoccupied with uttering religious quotations, during the first year or so of our work together I was able to collect significant data about his real-life experiences and connect their impact on his adult mental state.

Attis was the fourth child of a rather poor uneducated rural family. Both his father's and mother's ancestors had come to the United States from middle Europe long ago and had Germanic names, but

11

while Attis was growing up the family did not seem to have an obvious investment in any specific ethnic identity. There were no pictures of ancestors hanging on the walls of their farmhouse. A print in a wooden frame showing a bleeding Jesus on the cross stood on the mantle of the fireplace in the living room. Attis' parents were Methodists, Southern Americans who went to church on Sundays. Their church services were only for white people, and they blamed African-Americans for unsolved crimes. When they had time, they listened to country music on the radio. Attis' father earned his living by selling vegetables and fruit raised on the family's small farm, and his mother stayed home raising her children, although she also was required to help her husband by working in the fields.

As far as Attis knew, he had been a healthy infant. He was born on Groundhog Day, 2 February, which is also known as Candlemas Day. Attis knew that on Candlemas Day, forty days after Jesus' birth, his mother Mary presented him to God at the Temple in Jerusalem. When Attis was a child, however, the focus in the family was not on him becoming a future light as baby Jesus was. The focus was on the groundhog story that began as a Pennsylvania German custom in the United States in the eighteenth century (Yoder, 2003). It is said that on 2 February the groundhog comes out of hibernation. According to tradition, if the animal sees his shadow, he is frightened and retreats into his hole for another six weeks of winter weather. If he does not see his shadow, spring will come soon. When Attis was born, there was a terrible and devastating storm; the groundhog could not see his shadow and he did not return to his hole. But, in this case, the winter was not over. Attis' mother, by often repeating the story of the storm during his birth, made her son feel that the circumstances indicated a malignant destiny. Occasionally, child Attis identified himself with a groundhog and he was often filled with a sense of doom, which, in fact, was not incompatible with the events of his childhood.

Attis had two older brothers and one older sister. When he was twenty months old, his mother bore twins, a boy and a girl. As luck would have it, two other women in the neighbourhood gave birth to twins at about the same time and the three women became highly competitive about their offspring. His mother's preoccupation with the twins and with a deaf girl born a year after the twins arrived served to deprive Attis of adequate mothering in early childhood. Attis could not recall if he was breastfed or bottle fed when he was an infant. But he knew that, for a time, he carried a bottle with him and stayed in diapers along with the babies. Attis recalled how, while growing up, he had been regarded by others in the family as unduly tied to his mother's apron strings, but their "togetherness" was filled with tension and sadistic attacks by the mother, such as her screaming and telling him that he was a nuisance and that she was tired of his whining. He could not remember ever being hugged by his mother. Between the ages of three and four, Attis was involved in several severely traumatic episodes. His mother's role in these events further complicated her son's response to them and his finding his own healthy psychic individuation. On two separate occasions there were fires in his house, once while he was sick in bed with a high fever; his mother rescued him each time. When he was growing up his mother would remind him often that she was his "saviour" and that without her he would be dead.

Listening to Attis, I developed an image of his mother as a lonely, angry, and confused woman with seven children. She, I sensed, felt overwhelmed with mothering activities and work on the farm, especially after Attis' birth when she became pregnant with the twins and a year after their birth when she had a deaf baby. Attis' mother might have had an unconscious wish that Attis had perished in these fires. This way she would have had more time for herself and the other babies.

This might have been the reason why she would tell Attis, again and again, that without her presence he would not be alive. She might also have had unconscious guilt over her deficiencies in mothering Attis, as well as the possibility that her unconscious wish for his disappearance could become a reality. I concluded that Attis' mother was not able to help her son differentiate clearly between his internal state and external reality, to develop a sufficient capacity to "mentalise" (Fonagy & Target, 1996; Target & Fonagy, 1996). Attis could not accomplish a sufficient separation–individuation (Mahler, 1968) from the mental representation of his mother and he could not integrate the caring mother image with the image of his mother's frequent yelling at him. His mother would tell him that she would give him to an ugly, unmarried old woman in the rural area where they lived. This old woman was apparently a fortune teller and had a reputation for being a "bitch". Adult Attis imagined her as an ugly woman with a big nose and ugly teeth. He often thought that the "bitch" was an extension of his "bad" mother. Child Attis came to the oedipal age with mentalisation and unresolved separation–individuation problems.

The following story further illustrates Attis' mother's role in his difficulty differentiating between reality and fantasy, and in his separation–individuation issues. When he was four, Attis was helping his second older brother chop wood. With his right index finger, he pointed to a spot where he thought his brother should strike the axe. His brother chopped off his finger. When this happened, his mother put Attis in the family truck and rushed him to a doctor whose office was some distance away to have the severed piece sewn back in place. Her oft-repeated account of what actually happened indicated that in her panic she "forgot" to take the severed part with her; had she done so, the child might have had his finger restored. Instead, when they returned to the farm, she preserved the severed digit in some kind of liquid in a bottle.

I can only imagine Attis' mother's motivation for keeping her son's severed finger in a bottle. Perhaps she had a wish to get rid of her son/his finger but also wanted to deny her guilt for "forgetting" to take the cut segment of the finger to the doctor's office. Perhaps she was overwhelmed by having a handicapped baby daughter and did not wish to have a physically handicapped son and thus denied Attis becoming handicapped. Perhaps she had sexualised unconscious fantasies about the finger segment. Of course, I will never know for sure her psychological reasons for her unusual decision to keep the cut finger in a bottle.

Because the glass was transparent, anyone, including Attis, could see what was in the bottle. The mother was "proud" of this grim object, which she kept in the guestroom and often displayed to visitors. Because of how his mother related to the finger in the bottle, as a child Attis perceived it as "alive". His mother, just as she had had his life in her possession when she rescued him from the house fires, also possessed his "alive" finger. The child's finger stump was not yet healed when he had his first experience with surgery—a tonsillectomy. In the same year in which he had his first tonsillectomy, Attis fell off a ladder into a bin of cottonseed. On this occasion he could have suffocated and died. This time he managed to save himself.

When Attis described his father I surmised this man to be a sadistic individual who did not pay much attention to his children and who did not express love. He did not drink and only rarely physically abused his children, but he had frequent temper tantrums. Attis was afraid of his father's temper and often saw his father in a fury forcing a stick up a donkey's anus when the animal disobeyed his master's orders.

I concluded that the father did nothing to help little Attis become "unglued" from a "crazy mother", as Attis referred to her on several occasions.

When he was of oedipal age, Attis was told how a worker at a nearby farm went into a cave and severed his penis with a knife. When he told me about this event as an adult he trembled. In general he would not allow himself to express his emotions openly. As an oedipal-age child, he was preoccupied with the account of the farmworker's self-castration and felt menace in the environment. I suspected that in his mind the farmworker's self-castration was linked with his losing a segment of one of his fingers. Attis continued to believe that the finger in the bottle was "alive" and also stood for a penis. Since this time he had had fears about sharp objects. At the age of eight he sustained a back injury that not only left a physical scar on his hips but supported his belief that life is full of physical danger.

When Attis reached puberty, in the midst of his second individuation (Blos, 1979), his father had an appendectomy. Apparently, Attis' mother went to the hospital and managed to acquire her husband's appendix. She put it also in a bottle filled with the same kind of liquid that was supposed to preserve Attis' finger. She placed this bottle in the parental bedroom, brought Attis' finger from the guestroom and displayed them together. Again, I do not know what her psychological motivation was for doing such a thing. Attis gazed at the father's appendix and his own finger and concluded that the appendix was larger than the finger segment. He clearly recalled how he wished that the larger appendix belonged to him. He sometimes wished to eat his father's appendix and imagined that he had. Then he would have a stomachache or think that his father's eaten appendix would turn into a penis in his stomach.

I allowed my mind to wander and thought that Attis' fantasy to eat his father's appendix/penis, which was bigger than his finger segment, illustrated his wish to identify with his father in a most primitive fashion, by introjecting the father's penis in a *concrete* fashion, by "eating" it. His method for finding a way to unglue himself from his mother by introjecting (eating) his father/the father's penis, his "reaching up" (Boyer, 1961, 1983; Volkan, 1976, 1997, 2010) from pregenital conflicts to oedipal issues, would not work because of the father's scary sadism, especially his penetrating a donkey's anus with a stick; the internalised father might put a stick in his son's butt too!

Attis was good at athletic activities when they required no teamwork, such as running, competing individually. He was aware that he was different from his classmates and this prevented him from doing well scholastically. He had thoughts that he would not share with his friends. For example, sometimes he would "believe" that he had three penises. The first one was his real penis between his legs. The second one was represented by his finger segment in the bottle. It was not just a symbol for his penis, it *was* his castrated penis, but "alive". The third penis was in his stomach, his father's appendix. Sometimes he also thought that he had two vaginas, his two armpits. His vaginas, resembling his mother's vagina that he had seen, were divided into a "good" one and a bleeding and "bad" one. In short, he was a hermaphrodite being.

I imagined that his having three penises responded to a variety of things. The more penises Attis had, the more he could still possess one after being "castrated" by his brother/mother's agent and after expecting castration again, this time by his father. If he remained regressed and "fused" with his mother he should at least have two vaginas separating the "good" mother he wished to have from the "bad" one he had experienced again and again. He could not integrate his mother's mental representation. Perhaps he also wanted to have an extra vagina in case his father mutilated one by putting a stick in it.

As a teenager, after having dreams or fantasies of having sex with his mother, Attis would think of being sent to hell. He would easily associate his image of being in hell with his memories of the horror of twice being in a burning house and the feeling of suffocation from being buried alive in a bin of cottonseed. He recalled being so interred in his adult phobia. When Attis was twenty years old, he had severe pains in his stomach. He told me that, looking back, he was not sure if the pain was due to his fantasy of eating his father's appendix or due to a medical issue. His physician decided that Attis was suffering from acute appendicitis. He had surgery and his appendix was removed (but not saved by his mother). After his father died from heart failure when Attis was twenty-two years old, Attis believed that his father was buried alive and that he might come back and castrate him. Once when he was twenty-four and again when he was twenty-six Attis had throat surgery. In his mind the stomach-ache, the appendectomy, and the two throat surgeries seemed to be linked to the images of his childhood experiences.

His continuing fear of going to hell and being consumed by fire inspired Attis' wish to seek God. I sensed that "God" stood for parent figures that could not be "killed" or damaged by his rage against them. By turning to God he could save himself from experiencing overwhelming guilt feelings and fear of "bad" parents' retaliation. He seemed to have no religious calling in the usual sense and was very much conflicted in relating to the church, the image of which, I thought, was also fused intermittently with the mental representation of his mother. After much difficulty in a well-known college, he left for a second-class divinity school, and graduated at age 25. He was then a Methodist minister.

From what Attis told me and from reading his detailed medical records from a hospital where he had been taken two years after his graduation, I could piece together the story of his first major dramatic psychotic episode. At that time he had a ministerial position in a little country church. Listening to him, my thinking was that obtaining this position forced him to think of himself as an adult. But he could not function as an individuated male adult without identifying with a strong father figure or, at least, being an extension of him. His biological father was already dead. One Sunday while he was preaching in his church he felt that the congregation was looking at him in adoration. This was a "sign" informing him that he could turn into Jesus, God's son on earth. As the Virgin Mary presented her son to God on Candlemas day he himself could be presented to God as Jesus. There was only one woman in the church, a "bitch", who was the devil's agent. But, by becoming Jesus he could deal with her. On Monday morning Attis walked into the nearby deep woods, climbing to the mountaintop. As he walked, he tore his clothing from his slender, well-muscled body; there should be no barriers between him and his God. He was slashed by branches as he walked naked, and oozing blood made him look as though he had been savagely whipped. On the mountaintop, he threw out his arms as though he were nailed to the cross and stood motionless to receive his Father, whose power he felt in the rays of the hot summer sun that began to burn his torn body.

When it was realised that the twenty-seven-year-old minister was missing, a search party was sent after him. He was found three days later, naked, dehydrated, and nearly dead. Covered with dried blood and badly sunburned, he looked so much like an animal that the man who found him seized his right hand to make a positive identification, as it was common knowledge that the young minister had lost a finger on that hand.

Attis was taken to a hospital where he was diagnosed as suffering from schizophrenia. Following this hospitalisation, he was eventually allowed to return to his job. He was assigned to another rural area where, I surmised, religious belief and customs were unsophisticated, good and evil were seen as issues of black and white, and signs from beyond taken seriously. In such a milieu, Attis could conceal his delusions most of the time, making an adjustment to his environment. By this time his older siblings had moved away from North Carolina and married. The twins stayed near their parents and were involved in farming, but eventually they married as well. His deaf sister stayed in the same house with her mother and never married. As an adult, Attis had minimal contact with his siblings.

His mother wanted Attis to marry a woman she approved of. He met a schoolteacher, Gloria, in the new community where he was sent by the church after his dramatic psychotic episode and hospitalisation. His new location was not far away from the rural area where his mother still lived. His mother visited him, met Gloria, interviewed and approved her. She told her son that the younger woman would be a good wife to a Methodist minister as she seemed obedient, silent, and devoted to Christ. Until this point Attis had not made any sexual advances towards a woman. (Even though he had two "vaginas" he was never interested in sexual relationships with men.) He made plans to marry the schoolteacher, learning just before the marriage took place that she was not a virgin. She had had an affair with an older man, just as Attis suspected or fantasised that his mother had done in her girlhood. Attis recalled, even at this time, having the feeling that his mother and Gloria were interchangeable. Gloria confessed that indeed she had been an older man's lover before and while courting Attis, and that this man had later rejected her. While protesting the marriage in his mind, saying to himself that he was trapped, Attis went through with the marriage ceremony.

Attis would sometimes feel the presence of his father in the house he shared with his wife, locating this presence particularly in the closets, which at times he refused to open on this account. Sometimes he hallucinated his father's grinning face and adopted more psychological defences, shouting three times to it to leave him alone and becoming temporarily catatonic if the face remained. Attis was unable to leave home without dread of having left something burning inside the house; he compulsively checked the stove and all the locks each time he went out. As a married man he had a recurrent dream, reflecting his childhood accident in which his finger was cut off. In it, he saw a door drop like a guillotine on a snake and cut it into two pieces. Sometimes he hallucinated and saw guillotines and snakes in the house.

Attis' mother kept the severed finger in the bottle until her death when Attis was thirty-eight years old, a year before he became my patient. After his mother's death, Attis took the bottle with the finger in it to the home he was sharing with Gloria. He kept it in a dresser drawer and sometimes thought of it as living. The father's appendix in the bottle was left behind and was later lost. By this time, the finger in the bottle was mummified and shrunken; it was a dark piece of hard material. About six months after I had first met him Attis brought the finger in a bottle to one of his sessions in a heavy briefcase. He opened the briefcase, took out a bottle and showed the morbid item to me. There was no longer any liquid in the bottle, and indeed the thing in the bottle was an indistinguishable dried-up, dark object. I did not touch the bottle. He put it back into his briefcase and made sure that the briefcase was tightly closed. Later, Attis would tell me that after showing me the finger in the bottle he had returned it to the same dresser drawer. Its magic apparently continued.

After his mother's death and his possession of his dried-up finger segment, Attis' swings from extreme dependency upon his wife to extreme, but unexpressed, rage towards her increased. He began to show more signs and symptoms related to fusion of self- and object images or representations and/or one object image with another. While his experiences with fusion with other images or mental representations had existed before, they were temporary. (Here I am using the term "mental representation" as a collection of mental images.) Now, he could hardly differentiate Gloria from the mental representation of his mother. He was, however, able to differentiate himself from the mental representation of his wife. On occasions during the sex act he would think that he was his father. On many other occasions, making love to Gloria seemed to him as if he were involved in an incestuous relationship.

During sex, his body perception would change. Before orgasm, he would experience himself as a frog between Gloria's legs facing the mouth of a walrus, which I thought represented the concept of *vagina dentata*, a vagina that contains teeth. Putting a penis in a vagina that contains teeth might result in castration. I thought that the symbolism of the frog was connected with his idea of a detachable penis (the finger or the appendix in a bottle). Luis Cortés (1978) has noted a connection between frogs and genitalia in numerous paintings and sculptures from medieval and Renaissance Europe. When not intimate with Gloria, Attis was preoccupied with a longing for "freedom" from wife/mother. He wanted to divorce Gloria but never actually initiated such action.

When his primary process thinking dominated, in his mind his divorce/separation from his wife/mother as well as mourning over a person (his mother, who in reality had died) could be accomplished through the death of Gloria or himself. The psychological separation could only be achieved by the physical death of one of the partners. Mourning means a preoccupation with the mental images of the lost person or thing (Freud, 1917e; Volkan, 1981a; Volkan & Zintl, 1993). As long as a person is alive he will maintain the images of important lost objects. However, when there are no complications the mourning process comes to a practical end: the mental representation of the lost person or thing becomes "futureless" (Tähkä, 1984, 1993). The mourner no longer remains preoccupied with the images of the lost object. Attis could not mourn as a "normal" adult. For Attis, as the first anniversary of his mother's death approached, "finishing" his mourning over the dead mother literally meant "killing" the wife/mother. He was experiencing a complicated, psychotic "anniversary reaction" (Pollock, 1989). During this time he was called upon to perform an unusually large number of funeral services as a minister. He became more preoccupied with graveyards and the return of his dead parents. Sometimes at night he saw lights moving among the graves.

The night prior to the two policemen bringing him to North Carolina Memorial Hospital, as Gloria lay sleeping next to him, Attis recalled having the strongest impulse to kill her. Getting out of bed, he went to the backyard of the house and fetched an axe. He was very careful not to be seen by his dead father who might come from the cemetery. His finger was cut off by an axe and the brother who had cut off his finger was his mother's agent. Now, he aimed to do to his wife/mother what his brother had done to him. As he approached his sleeping wife, apparently he went into a catatonic state. He did not remember how he had stopped short of being a murderer.

Some years after I first met Attis, when I was a psychoanalytic candidate at the Washington Psychoanalytic Institute, one of my beloved teachers was Edith Weigert. She had studied various versions of the Attis (or Atys) myth (Weigert, 1938). When I wrote about my patient for the first time (Volkan, 1976) I gave him the name of Attis because this mythological figure's story focuses on the preservation of body parts, especially keeping a finger alive after death. Other themes of the myth of Attis also preoccupied my patient's mind, such as castration, hermaphroditism, incest, and drinking (eating) the Other's blood.

There are different versions of the myth of Attis, according to my reading of Greek mythology. As the story is told by Carl Kerényi (1980), the Agdos rock assumed the shape of the Great Mother. Zeus fell asleep on it and his semen caused the rock to deliver Agdistis, a hermaphrodite being of great savagery. In an effort to tame Agdistis, Dionysos turned water into wine, which the thirsty Agdistis drank until he fell into a deep sleep. Dionysos then tied the male member of the sleeping Agdistis to a tree, so that, when he sprang up from his sleep, he castrated himself. The earth drank the blood and ate the torn-off member and from these grew a new tree. Nana, the daughter of Sangarius, the river god, placed its fruit in her lap. She conceived a child of it and Sangarius left the infant out in the open to die, but a he-goat tended him and he survived. His name was Attis and his beauty was such that Agdistis, now without a male member, fell in love with him. Midas, King of Pessinous, sought to separate Attis from Agdistis and, to this end, gave the boy his own daughter in marriage. Agdistis appeared at the wedding and drove the guests mad with the notes of a syrinx, whereupon Attis castrated himself and died. Repentant, Agdistis besought Zeus to return the boy to life but all that Fate would allow was to grant that his body would never putrefy, his hair would continue to grow and his smallest finger would remain alive and capable of movement.

My patient's finger in the bottle was "alive", kept so, not by Zeus, but by the patient's mother. His mother was a soul murderer (Shengold, 1991) and had "killed" her son's soul, but made sure that his finger/penis would remain "alive".

CHAPTER THREE

My first three months with Attis

arly in my training in psychiatry I developed a habit of keeping notes on my work with patients whose cases, I thought, would give me illustrations of psychodynamic concepts and whom I considered as "special". Attis was certainly a special patient for me. While writing this book, decades after my first meeting with him, I primarily depended on my notes and what I had written about him in my two previous books, *Primitive Internalized Object Relations* (Volkan, 1976) and *The Infantile Psychotic Self and its Fates* (1995). I do not have extensive notes on my work with him during his first hospitalisation at the North Carolina Memorial Hospital, which lasted three months, but I do have some vivid memories.

During his hospitalisation I visited Attis every working day and spent fifty minutes with him each visit. During the initial three weeks of his stay at the hospital, except on the first day of his hospitalisation, he did not talk with me. Whenever I entered his room I found him sitting on a chair hiding beneath the blanket he had taken from his bed and pulled over his head. According to the nurses he spent most of his time hidden in this manner. The nurses told me that Attis would leave his room for meals, but he would suddenly scurry back.

23

The psychiatrist in charge of the inpatient unit would meet with psychiatry residents who had patients in the inpatient unit, nurses, and social workers every day except on weekends. I would also see my older colleague once a week for private supervision. At the direction of my supervisor, I was having full fifty-minute sessions with Attis even when he did not speak. I was supposed to listen to my patient's "silences". For an inexperienced therapist this was difficult, and it was much later when I would learn about different types of "silences" that patients exhibit on the couch. Peter, the animal killer, whose case I referred to in the introduction to this book, had gone through a very long silent period during his analysis, session after session. Patients like him who possess a narcissistic personality organisation often escape into a "cocoon" (Modell, 1975; Rudden, 2011) or a "glass bubble" (Volkan, 1979a, 2010, 2014a) on the couch as an expression of their grandiose fantasy of living alone in a kingdom and needing no one. Sometimes while inside their "glass bubble" they do not need to speak. Another type of patient, an overtly dependent one, may stay silent, comfortable, satisfied, and secure when he develops an intense transference of being like a baby in the arms of a loving analyst/mother (Volkan, 2014a). Other times, a patient with rage does not speak when she feels that her words will act like bullets.

Attis did not have a narcissistic personality organisation with a lonely kingdom, but a psychotic one. His silences did not indicate that he was feeling comfortable, satisfied, and safe in my arms. My supervisor and I concluded that Attis' hiding behind a blanket and remaining silent in the foetal position was primarily a concrete illustration of his regression into a womb. Because of his difficulty with reality testing and differentiating between thoughts/affects, he would stay in a "womb" in order to deal with intolerable anxiety. He also feared that once more he might surrender to his murderous impulses if he believed that his words, as bullets, might harm me.

The supervisor helped those working with Attis to remain non-intrusive, and we tried to present a safe environment for the Methodist minister. I recall being told how a new therapist should always remember that being together with a patient is not like being with someone in a social setting and that the therapist needs to develop a "therapeutic identity" or, in Stanley Olinick's words, become a "therapeutic instrument" (Olinick, 1980). Trying to develop a "therapeutic identity", following my supervisor's advice, I would tell Attis that I was in the room listening to his silences and that he could speak whenever he was ready to do so. I added that he and I would be curious about his thoughts when he verbalised them. I was not directed to give any kind of medicine to patients, but to learn about their psychological conflicts and deficiencies, and respond to them psychotherapeutically. In fact, throughout the decades that I would work with Attis I never gave him any medicine and he never asked for any. I followed my supervisor's suggestions and after three weeks the Methodist minister started to tell me about himself, at first in a piecemeal and bizarre fashion.

This began in the following way. One day, after I told Attis that I would not harm him if he would emerge from beneath the blanket, Attis put his fingers out from under the blanket and wiggled them. He then began talking while still hiding. I thought that he was showing me that he was missing a finger. At that time I did not know the story of how he had lost it. As he had during our first meeting, he began citing biblical passages, none of which were familiar to me. The next day he began talking to me without hiding behind his blanket. He referred to himself as a "monster" with three penises and two vaginas. He hallucinated snakes in the room; he did not fear them but feared their being hurt. He talked about a guillotine cutting a snake into two pieces. Such observations convince a beginning therapist that a snake is a symbol of a penis.

One day Attis began to insist that he was a groundhog. At that time I did not know enough English and I did not know what a groundhog was. It would take many months before I learned the folklore of Groundhog Day and of Attis' birth on that day. Today, I appreciate the hard task that many International Psychoanalytic Association supervisors face when they supervise candidates from countries where psychoanalytic training is new. Not knowing the language, history, folklore, and mythology that exist in places such as China, Korea, Turkey, or Bulgaria where the establishment of psychoanalytic training is still ongoing, makes supervision of local candidates' therapeutic work a challenge. Looking back I think that my not knowing biblical references and what the word groundhog meant was most likely useful during the very initial phase of my work with the Methodist minister. I was literally a "blank slate" to which he could externalise aspects of himself and project his affects and bizarre thoughts without my complicating them and then returning them to him.

During Attis' three-month stay at the North Carolina Memorial Hospital Gloria came to see Rebecca once a week with the aim of understanding her husband's illness and to learn to "manage" him better after his release from the hospital. The social worker would meet with me regularly and tell me about her meetings with Gloria. I learned that Gloria had no close relatives nearby, but had several female friends whom she could call on quickly when she needed support and advice. She also had a direct line to an authority in the Methodist Church. Having a steady profession seemed to give her self-esteem, but Rebecca and I sensed her masochistic tendencies; she seemed to express guilt feelings for having had an affair with an older man. This affair apparently continued even after she was engaged to be married to Attis. Rebecca explained to me how when she had her affair Gloria was "acting out" her childhood oedipal fantasies which were overtly stimulated and complicated by her childhood experiences, including having had a father who sometimes drank and walked around naked at home while making sexual remarks about his pre-teenage daughter. Rebecca sensed that Gloria was still feeling guilty and was determined to be a "good wife" to the Methodist minister, even though he was strange and dangerous. Gloria did not want to have children and made sure that she would not get pregnant. Each time she came to visit Rebecca she would also spend time with her husband.

The combination of nurses' and my efforts to create a secure environment for Attis at the university hospital, and Gloria's visits helped him to become more relaxed. Sometimes he appeared to be a "normal" individual and exhibited social skills in relating to other inpatients and hospital personnel. During our sessions he described his life experiences in a routine way, but would still sometimes suddenly ask me if I were Pastor Johns, his father, or his mother in disguise. Sometimes he would behave as though I *was* Pastor Johns, his father, or his mother. His various object images would become fused and interchangeable. Occasionally, he would give me murderous looks and threaten to kill me. I guess I was too naïve or inexperienced to feel frightened.

Much later in my career I would write about establishing a "reality base" (Volkan, 1995, 2010) during the initial part of a therapeutic relationship with individuals who have psychotic conditions and break with reality. Anna Freud (1954) noted that neurotic patients' attitudes toward their analysts as they enter analysis are already based on reality. A person suffering from a neurosis has fantasies about the therapist (and in turn the therapist has fantasies about the patient) even before the two meet for the first time (Volkan, 2010). But a patient with a neurotic condition has no difficulty in separating what is real from what is not real. She knows that her therapist or analyst is *not* her mother, father, sibling, or another important individual. Making practical arrangements for meeting times and payments will be enough to establish a reality base. Later, such a patient will build a transference neurosis on this reality base. A person suffering from psychosis has overt and covert extreme transference distortions as treatment begins. The therapist or the analyst needs to establish a reality base from the beginning.

When Attis fused my image with his dead mother or father I would simply remind him that I was not his mother or father. A therapist's reliance on what Finnish psychoanalyst Veikko Tähkä (1984, 1993) called "empathic description" supports the development of a reality base for patients like Attis at the very beginning of their treatment. Tähkä re-examined the classic concept of "interpretation", defined as bringing to the patient's awareness mental conflicts and their contents that were previously unconscious. He stated that the classical definition of interpretation links it with the phenomena of repression and dynamic unconscious. Therefore, interpretation as a therapeutic tool can be utilised only for those patients with neurotic pathology whose main defence mechanism is repression. Interpretation in the classical sense could not correspond to the subjective experience of a patient like the Methodist minister, even when he might grasp an interpretation intellectually. An individual like the Methodist minister will not respond to interpretation. Such a patient will most likely respond to the therapist's catching and describing the patient's way of experiencing in a method that is analogous to a primary developmental object's (i.e., mother's) understanding of her offspring and conveying that understanding to the patient (empathic description). I would explain to Attis that he was bringing his unfinished psychological struggles with his parents to our relationship and then feeling as though he were actually reliving his childhood. Even though he did not really understand what I was describing, I noticed that he felt more at ease by sensing that I knew what his trouble was. I tried to remain as a steady "Other" who would help him to test the reality, especially when he seemed to be frightened of being flooded with high anxiety and murderous feelings.

I will now report on some events in my own background and make some remarks about my supervisor in the service of illustrating how a therapist's and even a supervisor's personal issues contaminate a therapist's interactions with a patient, as aspects of the patient's history, behaviour patterns, and symptoms awaken some psychological issues in the therapist. For three months I sensed or fantasised that my supervisor stood by me and supported me more than other fellow psychiatry residents on the same inpatient unit. I liked this and also found it a familiar situation. Let me explain. The Ottoman Turks conquered the island of Cyprus in 1571. My mother's family belonged to the Ottoman elite when Cyprus was still an Ottoman island, and her wealthy grandfather was the *kadı* (religious chief judge) of Nicosia, the capital city. In 1878 the Ottoman Sultan "rented" the island to the British in order to secure British support for the Ottomans' struggle with the Russians. The British wanted to be in Cyprus to protect their interest in the Suez Canal. Although Cyprus remained nominally Ottoman territory during this period, it was formally annexed by the British in 1914 at the start of World War I, in which the Ottoman Empire allied itself with Imperial Germany. Modern-day Turkey formally recognised British rule in Cyprus in 1923, and the island became a crown colony the following year.

In 1878, after the island was rented and British administration was established in Nicosia, my great-grandfather lost his position, and this lead to marital difficulties. His son, my maternal grandfather, obviously frustrated, did not follow in his father's footsteps to become a well-known respected and highly intellectual figure of the community; instead, he lived on comfortably using the family's existing financial assets until they dwindled. Slowly the family lost its prestige and also its financial status. One of my mother's brothers was named after his *kadı* grandfather. I suspect that unconsciously he was given the task to bring back the family's prestigious name and fortune. He was thought to be, whether true or not, a "genius". When he was a young university student in Istanbul his dead body was found in the Marmara Sea some fifty days after he had disappeared. After I became a psychoanalyst I suspected that my "genius" uncle was under great pressure to bring back the family's prestige and that this pressure was one major reason for his committing suicide. When I was born, the family gave me the name of my dead uncle and my *kadı*, great-grandfather. What was important was my being a "replacement child" (Cain & Cain, 1964; Legg & Sherick, 1976; Green & Solnit, 1964; Poznanski, 1972; Ainslie & Solyom, 1986; Volkan & Ast, 1997).

My mother and grandmother deposited into my self-representation the idealised mental representation of my dead uncle and tasks originally given to him. Depositing (Volkan, 1987, 2010; Volkan, Ast & Greer, 2002), like identification, is utilised by a child for the development of his personality characteristics. In identification, the child is the primary active partner in taking in and assimilating an adult's mental images and owning this person's ego and superego functions. In depositing, the adult person more actively pushes specific images into the developing self-representation of the child and assigns psychological tasks to the deposited images. In other words, the adult person uses the child (mostly unconsciously) as a permanent reservoir for certain self- and other images and psychological tasks belonging to such images. Melanie Klein's (1946) "projective identification" can explain such a process. However, I wish to use the term "depositing" to illustrate how parenting individuals create a psychological DNA in the child. Anne Ancelin Schützenberger's (1998) "ancestor syndrome", Judith Kestenberg's (1982) term "transgenerational transposition", and Haydée Faimberg's (2005) description of "the telescoping of generations" refer to depositing traumatised images.

An adult's depositing an image in the developing child's self-representation, as well as a child's identification with an adult's image, takes place silently. Nevertheless, there were some visible signs of my being a replacement child. For example, I had to be "number one" in my class at the end of each school year while attending middle and high school, otherwise my mother and grandmother would have "depression" during the summer. Usually I was able to achieve this. Transgenerational transmission of a psychological task forced me to develop a strong and, I believe and hope, healthy narcissism. I learned of my being a "replacement child" partly during my personal analysis and later through self-analysis and collection of historical data about my family. I believe that as a child I assimilated the combined idealised images of my uncle and my elite Ottoman ancestor, traumatised by a historical event, into my self-representation. My being driven to be a "rescuer" of my family's fame or fortune, and my ability to sublimate, I believe, played a role in my becoming a psychoanalyst (Volkan, 1985). So, in the late 1950s my supervisor's attention to me and his interest in me as if I were "number one" among my fellow psychiatry residents, and my becoming a "rescuer" of Attis felt familiar. All I needed to learn was to "rescue" a patient through a therapeutic methodology.

There was another, most likely a more important, reason for my initial devotion in Attis' case and later for my keeping him as my patient for decades. I became fully aware of this reason only years after I started to work with Attis. Here follows the story of my second motivation for my devotion to Attis' case.

During the last two and a half years of my life in Ankara before I came to the United States in early 1957 I shared a small room in an apartment complex with another Cypriot Turk named Erol Mulla. He had come to Ankara, as had I, for his medical education and was two classes below me at the same medical school. He called me *abi* meaning "my big brother". Since I only had sisters and no brothers, I considered him to be my brother. During the time we were roommates ethnic conflict began between the Cypriot Turks and Cypriot Greeks. Three months after my arrival in the United States I received a letter from my father. In the envelope there was a newspaper article with Erol's picture describing how he had gone to Cyprus from Ankara to visit his ailing mother. While trying to purchase medicine for her at a pharmacy he was shot seven times by a Cypriot Greek terrorist. This person killed Erol, a bright young man with a promising future, in order to terrorise the ethnic group to which he belonged.

After receiving the news of Erol's death I felt numb. I did not cry. I was in Chicago in a foreign environment in which I was close to no one, so I did not share the news of Erol's murder with any other person. Even when I was undergoing my personal analysis some years later, I did not dwell on losing Erol. My "hidden" mourning process, I believe, largely remained just that—hidden. As a young analyst I felt close to the late William Niederland and, in a sense, I thought of him as a mentor even though he lived in New York City and I lived in Charlottesville, Virginia. At the time it never occurred to me that my seeking out William Niederland who had coined the term "survivor syndrome" (Niederland, 1968) as a mentor might have something to do with my losing Erol and my own "survival guilt". I published a book called *Cyprus: War and Adaptation* (Volkan, 1979b) in which I briefly described Erol's murder. During the same year I began my involvement in international affairs (Volkan, 2013). Then, after working with Arabs and Israelis for over six years, I was involved in bringing together Soviets and Americans, and later Russians and Estonians, and representatives of other opposing large groups to find peaceful solutions for their large-group problems. At the same time, I was trying to understand the psychology of ethnic, national, religious, or ideological conflicts that are associated with massive losses. Without being aware of my motivation, early in my career as a psychiatrist and psychoanalyst I devoted years to studying ethnic conflicts, mourning, and adaptation (Volkan, 1979b, 1981a, 2007a, 2007b; Volkan & Zintl, 1993).

Some thirty years after Erol's death I once more visited Cyprus. One summer night some friends took me to a garden restaurant, and one of them who knew Erol's story pointed out a bearded man behind the bar and told me that this man was Erol's younger brother. I spontaneously got up from my chair and approached this man and said to him, "My name is Vamık. Does this name mean anything to you?" He began to cry and I found myself also crying out loud, right in the midst of people dining, with soothing classical music playing in the background. This event activated my mourning process, which lasted many, many months. This time I was very aware of it.

It is clear that my hidden perennial mourning process and my readiness to give sublimated responses to it existed when I met Attis. Now, decades later, I can state that by devoting my interest to treating a potential murderer I unconsciously wished to understand why people kill other people. With this understanding, most likely, I wanted to change potential murderers' internal worlds and stop them from killing people. In my case, by treating Attis, I wanted to keep Erol Mulla alive!

I used to think that my supervisor's attitude towards me was due to his fascination with having a patient on his inpatient unit who was a potential wife killer. As I write this book now another thought has come to my mind about my supervisor. The chairman of the Department of Psychiatry had also lost a finger. When there was interest about my presenting Attis' case during one of the department's weekly case conferences that was open to all faculty members, psychiatry residents, and nursing staff, my supervisor prevented the presentation. He indicated that talking about a patient's cut finger in front of the chairperson might make the "boss" uncomfortable. I had no history of how the chairman had lost his finger; it was a mystery to me. Did my supervisor's investment in Attis' case have something to do with his wondering about the chairman's response to losing his finger? What was my supervisor's relationship with the chairman?

It is clear that some of my personal issues were connected with my early work with Attis, although I was then not aware of them. If such connections become available to a therapist he must think about how such connections may influence the therapeutic process. The topic of countertransference should not remain simply as a theoretical concept.

Sometimes, aspects of the therapist's or analyst's countertransference remain hidden, and this was the situation while I was working with Attis, at least during the initial years of our relationship. In presenting total stories of therapeutic processes it is important, however, to report therapist's or analyst's personal issues that influence their investment in treatment processes in good or bad ways. I believe that in the long run my issues were helpful in my staying with Attis for decades and this was, in turn as we will see, very helpful to him.

After staying at North Carolina Memorial Hospital for three months Attis was discharged. Obviously, he was not well, but sufficiently organised to return to his daily life while clinging on to Gloria. He resumed his work as the Methodist minister of his community. He began to come to Chapel Hill once a week to have sessions with me. Before I give details of my therapeutic work with him after his first three-month hospitalisation at the North Carolina Memorial Hospital I will examine the following issues in the next three chapters:

- The impact of a childhood injury to a body part that symbolises a penis and its role in the evolution of an "actualised unconscious fantasy"
- The personality organisation of a person like Attis
- Typical psychological factors in the development of a psychotic core.

CHAPTER FOUR

A childhood injury to a body part that stands for a penis and actualised unconscious fantasy

How fear of physical injury develops throughout childhood and adolescence, in both boys and girls, has been reviewed by Jerome Blackman. He tells us: "When we speak of fear of physical injury, we are dealing both with reality and fantasy. Sometimes it is difficult to distinguish between the two" (Blackman, 2014, p. 123). He reminds us that some causes of fear of physical injury are identical in girls and boys. When children begin walking they become aware that when they fall, they get hurt. They also become aware that they can be physically hurt by someone else, such as a sibling who pushes them down. Blackman adds that while going through the separation–individuation phase (Mahler, 1968; Mahler, Pine & Bergman, 1975) children, both girls and boys, also share a similar fear of physical injury. When they experience aggression in the service of psychic separation from their mothers and other mothering persons they develop the capacity to fear that other persons who are targets for their aggressive feelings, in turn, can harm them. Blackman then illustrates how fear of physical injury in girls and boys is also dissimilar when the fear is linked to fantasies involving sexual organs. When little girls finger their vaginas, realise an "inner canal" and learn that babies come through this canal, they develop the fear that they can be hurt. Of course each girl's handling of this fear and the fantasy associated with it will be different owing to many factors. As Blackman states, many girls deny such "vulnerability". Boys begin to finger their genitals for pleasure just before the age of two. Blackman states: "By age three, their competitive feelings toward either parent will likely be projected, so that either parent is feared, even if the parents are gentle. For boys, the witnessing of the female genitalia (mother undressing, or girls being diapered during play groups) creates a thought of being without their pendulous penis. This thought adds to what is dramatically referred to as 'castration anxiety'" (Blackman, 2014, pp. 123–124).

Castration anxiety is fear of loss of, or injury to, a penis. In 1905 Sigmund Freud thought that castration anxiety was due to external traumatic threats. Later, he noticed that even in cases in which there is no such threat, the male child will still have a fantasy of castration (Freud, 1916–1917). As he imagines that girls are castrated, the little boy fears that he can be castrated too. He fears that his father will punish him for his oedipal wishes for his mother by castrating him. The boy suppresses or represses his oedipal longing for his mother and internalises his father's image as his superego. Freud also suggested that little girls develop penis envy and a feeling of inferiority due to not having a penis.

Today, Freud's ideas about castration fantasies in girls is questioned or rejected (see, for example, Bernstein, 1990). In our clinical practice however, we often notice that our adult male patients with neurotic personality organisation—even without a history of traumatic threats or injuries to their penises or body parts that represent a penis—express castration fantasies. Usually, such fantasies are unconscious, and only through therapeutic work do patients become aware of them. I presented the total psychoanalytic process of a patient I call Gable to illustrate in great detail the appearance of castration anxiety (Volkan, 2010). When Gable was three and a half years old his father was sent to a faraway island in the Pacific Ocean on military duty where he stayed for a little over a year. When his father was away, Gable slept with his mother in the parental bed. When his father returned he shared the bed with Gable's mother and the boy was "forced" to sleep alone in another room. The mother used to smoke cigarettes without telling her husband. She would come to her son's room in early evening to put little Gable to sleep. She would close her son's bedroom door, open a window, and smoke a cigarette sitting on the boy's bed, rubbing her son's hair to help him get to sleep while whispering, "This [her smoking a cigarette] is our secret. Do not tell your father." When Gable told me this story for the first time he made a slip of the tongue. He was referring to how his mother's smoking was like burning "incense" in his bedroom, but instead he said that the room was filled with "incest." It appears that his mother's sharing a "secret" with him while she was putting him to bed exaggerated Gable's castration anxiety. When he was twenty-four years old and studying English literature at the University of Virginia he became my analysand. Two years before we started working together, his father, then a general in the United States Armed Forces, had moved with Gable's mother and younger sister to a foreign country where he had been assigned. During the two years when his family was away, Gable remained in the United States and secretly married. Then he received a telegram from his father stating that he, his wife, and his daughter were getting ready to return to the United States. Gable became aware that he could no longer keep his marriage a secret and that his father would know that his son was using his penis for sexual intercourse. Gable became involved in various self-castration activities. For example, he quit his studies and became a road worker, getting cuts and bruises in the course of his workday. When he started his analysis with me his main preoccupation was to show me bleeding cuts on his arms and legs: he was already "castrated"; his analyst would have no need to castrate him!

When a male patient develops an oedipal transference neurosis, he may experience his analyst as a competitor for the love of a woman, such as a young female secretary who works at a place near the analyst's office. At the same time, the patient may evolve bodily symptoms and start visiting several physicians to find out what is wrong with his body, although in reality he suffers from no bodily ailment. He may dream about his analyst carrying a gun (a symbol of a penis) bigger than the gun he is carrying. Furthermore, the patient's own gun does not function well; it is broken. Going through such periods during an analytic process eventually makes the patient aware of his childhood castration fantasy.

Attis' finger was cut off "accidentally" by one of his brothers when Attis was four years old. He most likely experienced fear of physical injury before his finger was cut off, but after experiencing actual bodily harm, in child Attis' unconscious fantasy the cut finger became a cut penis. With the help of his mother's bizarre behaviour—keeping the severed finger in a bottle—Attis' castration fantasy became "real". Before examining the details of Attis' "actualised" unconscious fantasy I will examine theoretical and clinical aspects of unconscious fantasies in general.

Sigmund Freud described two types of unconscious fantasies: "Unconscious phantasies have been unconscious all along and have been formed in the unconscious; or—as is more often the case—they were once conscious phantasies, day-dreams, and have been purposely forgotten and have become unconscious through 'repression'" (Freud, 1908a, p. 161). The first type is usually conceptualised as inherited representations of the instinctual drives. Melanie Klein (1946, 1948) and her followers have given us illustrations of this type, such as a child's fantasy about a "bad breast". Here, my focus is on a type of unconscious fantasy that resembles Freud's second type of unconscious fantasy and is similar to Jacob Arlow's (1969) and Theodore Shapiro's (1990) descriptions of it: a child making an "interpretation" of an external event that reflects dreads or wishes and defences associated with such dreads and wishes according to the phase-specific oral, anal, phallic, and genital preoccupations associated with related affects and ego functions available to him, and also contaminating this "interpretation" with primary process thinking. A small girl who is traumatised by witnessing an aggressive primal scene may develop an unconscious fantasy that, when naked and holding each other, a man eats a woman.

Many psychoanalysts noticed that a repressed or sometimes dissociated "mental content", the unconscious fantasy, exerts an interminable psychodynamic effect on subsequent perceptions, affects, behaviour, thinking, responses to reality, and adaptive or maladaptive compromise formations (Beres, 1962; Sandler & Nagera, 1963; Arlow, 1969; Silverman, 1979; Inderbitzin & Levy, 1990; Shapiro, 1990, 2008). In psychoanalytic treatment, when the influence of this mental content on the patient become observable, then the patient and the analyst develop a "storyline" that transfers the unconscious fantasy into a formed thought process. Once the storyline of an unconscious fantasy is found, the unconscious fantasy then resembles an ordinary conscious fantasy or daydream, but remains illogical due to its absorption of primary process thinking.

Most unconscious fantasies concern themselves with body functions—such as eating, defecating, and having an erection—birth, death, sex, aggression, early object relations, separation–individuation, oedipal issues, physical injury, castration, family romance, mother's pregnancy, father's penis, and siblings.

Some unconscious fantasies are common. For example, Ast and I, in our book on siblings (Volkan & Ast, 1997) illustrated the commonality of various types of sibling-related womb fantasies. Such fantasies were described by Bertrand Levin as long ago as 1935. He illustrated how some womb fantasies underlie claustrophobia. A storyline of a womb fantasy could be: "I want to be my mother's only child in her womb. I will enter there and kill my unborn sibling, but my sibling in turn may kill me." An adult under the influence of such an unconscious fantasy, obviously without knowing why, may have anxiety about entering caves or may do the opposite and visit caves regularly. Caves symbolically represent a mother's womb without the person being aware of the psychological reason for either a hobby as a cave explorer or anxiety when entering a cave.

Since this book describes the case of a potential murderer, I will now briefly describe the story of a woman who, as a child, had a death wish towards a sister and an unconscious fantasy of being a murderer. In her case, dealing with the influence of an unconscious fantasy in adulthood was sublimated primarily by utilisation of reaction formation. When new events in her external world reactivated circumstances in her childhood that led to the formation of her unconscious fantasy, her sublimation broke down. The story of this woman, Amanda, was presented by Piyale Comert (2006).

Exhibiting preoccupation with her physical health, Amanda started her analysis at the age of thirty-nine, the age her mother had been when she died. Piyale Comert tells us how Amanda had a sister four years her senior. The sister had Noonan's syndrome and therefore a heart defect that required frequent hospitalisations until she had successful heart surgery at the age of thirteen. On many occasions when her sister was hospitalised, child Amanda would be left alone in the cafeteria of the hospital and would feel unloved. As she verbalised again and again during her analysis, Amanda patiently waited "for my turn" to be noticed and loved. She recalled how she, at age three, had thrown her sister's Barbie doll out the window of the car during a family trip. During her childhood, she often wished her sister would be kidnapped by gypsies. Eventually, Amanda and her analyst would openly verbalise Amanda's unconscious death wish for her sister and her unconscious fantasy of being a murderer. Amanda's parents' anxiety about the possibility of losing their oldest daughter during her hospitalisations played a role in supporting Amanda's wish and fantasy that her sister would disappear.

Adult Amanda's primary way of adapting to her unconscious fantasy and related guilt was through reaction formation. After her sister, who was married, gave birth to a son, he was diagnosed with having a more severe version of Noonan's than his mother's. Amanda did everything to "steal" this boy from her sister and take care of him. Her unconscious fantasy about getting rid of her sister was replaced by her becoming the saviour of her nephew. While the boy was growing up she lavished him with gifts and other generosities. When the boy turned eighteen, most likely due to his wish to individuate away from his aunt and also perhaps due to being prompted by his mother, he refused to accept his aunt's monthly financial aid. This event broke down Amanda's adaptation to her childhood unconscious fantasy and she felt depressed.

Piyale Comert (2006) states: "Around this time, she [Amanda] had a dream: Amanda goes into a cave to investigate what is inside and a ferocious animal/monster reaches out trying to grab her. We understood this dream as Amanda trying to reclaim her mother's womb and being greeted by her ferocious sister who stakes claim to the mother by blocking Amanda's access. The monster is also Amanda herself inside her mother and spewing terror." Amanda's nephew's refusal of her financial help and her womb dream occurred one year after Amanda' mother's death and just as her father was starting to date a young woman. Once more, Amanda's "turn to be noticed and loved" did not materialise. All these events placed Amanda at the mercy of the influence of her unconscious fantasy. As Gabriele Ast and I wrote: "One cannot stop murderous rage and associated unconscious fantasies by conscious decisions, nor can one control the effectiveness and reliability of reaction formations or sublimations" (Volkan & Ast, 1997, p. 73).

There are unconscious fantasies that are highly individualised; they belong *only* to the individual that has them. This occurs especially if the initiation of the unconscious fantasy is due to an unusual specific trauma or a collection of such traumas. For example, Gabriele Ast and I (Volkan & Ast, 2001) described the case of Gitta, who was born with a life-threateningly defective body. Beginning in infancy and lasting until she was nineteen years old, she endured forty surgical interventions. When she was born, Gitta was literally leaking from her mouth; her saliva had to be wiped out often in order to keep her alive, a task that her mother performed throughout Gitta's early childhood, as well as later when Gitta had to remain immobilised, sometimes for months, after some of her surgeries. As an infant, Gitta had been tube-fed, requiring a "hole" to be made in her body. And, throughout her childhood, the various surgical procedures and additional periods of tube feeding required countless additional openings to be made in her young body. Yet, when she started analysis in her late twenties with Dr. Ast, her physical appearance was for all practical purposes normal.

Gitta was exposed to the reality that as long as she bled or some other fluid (urine, faeces) came out of her body, she was not dead. Her unconscious fantasy was that she had a leaking body and that as long as her body leaked she was alive. The content of her unconscious fantasy could be seen rather openly in some of her conscious behaviour and thinking. For example, as an adult, she wore sanitary napkins every day since she "believed" that her menstrual flow was constant. She hesitated entering a swimming pool and avoided swimming in a nearby lake; later in analysis, it became apparent that she was afraid that the pool or lake water would enter her body through its "holes" and contaminate her own fluids. Her unconscious fantasy was actualised.

Actualisation of an unconscious fantasy (Volkan, 2004b, 2010; Volkan & Ast, 2001) occurs when the actual trauma is severe or a series of actual traumas are accumulated, and when they interfere with "the usual restriction of fantasy only or mostly to the psychological realm" (Volkan & Ast, 2001, p. 569). The individual continues to experience symbols or objects of displacement representing various aspects of the actualised fantasies as "protosymbols" (Werner & Kaplan, 1963). That is to say, to this individual, they *are* what in actuality they represent. In Gitta's case her actualised unconscious fantasy was highly individualised. I do not know of another woman who believes that her menstrual flow is constant and that her body is constantly leaking.

Sometimes common unconscious fantasies, shared by others, may also become actualised in an individual case. A girl's unconscious oedipal fantasy, in a routine developmental process, remains in the psychological realm and it will psychologically influence the individual as an adult according to the individual's capacity for repression and sublimation to one degree or another. If the influence of the girl's unconscious fantasy that is related to her wish to possess her father is very strong and not well sublimated, she, as an adult, may have a tendency to marry an older man (a father figure) or several older men one after another. Nevertheless, her unconscious fantasy still stays within the psychological realm. But if, while developing an unconscious oedipal fantasy, the little girl is severely traumatised, such as by being sexually assaulted by her father or a father substitute like an uncle or a priest, her unconscious oedipal fantasy may become "actualised". Because there is a strong link between the unconscious fantasy and reality, the little girl's unconscious fantasy will exist in *both* the psychological and experiential realms. During her adult sexual relations, the actualised unconscious fantasy, as the heir of her severe traumatic childhood event, can be experienced as "real", or at least partly real, and exist- ing in the present time. For example, if a man makes sexual advances towards her, most of the time or on some occasions, she can experience this man as the original traumatising and victimising father, uncle, or priest, even though in reality the man's advances remain within socially acceptable patterns. The man is not someone behaving *like* the origi- nal assaulting person; in the patient's mind, he *is* the assaulting per- son. If Piyale Comert's patient Amanda's sister had died in childhood, Amanda might have developed an actualised unconscious fantasy that she was a murderer.

Besides incest or repeated sexual stimulation by parents or others, malignant sibling rivalry, severe bodily injuries, surgeries, near-death experiences, drastic object losses, and exposure to massive destructions caused by events such as earthquakes or wars during childhood make a child prone to developing actualised unconscious fantasies. Severe actual trauma or accumulation of such traumas in early childhood may lead to developmental ego defects in mental structuring. Whenever there are ego defects, such as not being able to utilise differentiation among various self- or object images, or integration of them and repres- sion of certain affects effectively, there are also object-relations conflicts. In other words, as an adult the individual will experience tension or, as often is the case, severe anxiety concerning differentiating self-images from object images as well as integrating or not integrating libidinally and aggressively loaded self- and object images within, or externalising them on to others and re-internalising them. I do not separate such indi- viduals into those having only ego defects or only early object-relations conflicts. Such individuals' actualised unconscious fantasies reflect both ego defects and early object-relations conflicts and link them. When such a person's adult life is dominated extensively by actualised unconscious fantasy, that person will exhibit a clear break with reality. This situation applies to Attis' case.

At other times, we meet patients who separate and isolate a traumatised self-image with its corresponding object images and affects from the rest of more developed self-representation and thus dissociate their typical or actualised unconscious fantasies. What they do is known as "encapsulation" (D. Rosenfeld, 1992; H. Rosenfeld, 1965; see also Brenner, 2001, 2004). Encapsulation may break down, especially when an adult patient becomes involved in an event that closely reflects the theme of the original trauma. If encapsulation breaks down, the rest of the individual's self-system will be assaulted by the previously separated and isolated part, which may also include a previously "hidden" typical or actualised unconscious fantasy. When a previously actualised unconscious fantasy emerges from its "envelope", the individual may experience overwhelming tension and a limited or more generalised break with reality.

There is one more condition that is related to an unusual outcome for unconscious fantasies. Under certain circumstances a previously typical unconscious fantasy may become like an actualised one. For example, a man who had a murderous unconscious fantasy about his sibling in his mother's belly became a cave explorer as an adult. He had sublimated the influence of his typical unconscious fantasy through developing a hobby. One day he unexpectedly found a dead body in a cave. His fantasy was thus actualised in his adulthood (Volkan & Ast, 1997).

In this chapter I will not dwell further on unconscious fantasies that become actualised in adulthood since this topic is not related to Attis' case. Attis' actualised unconscious fantasy of being castrated had evolved when he was a child. Attis is not the only person I studied whose finger was cut off by an older brother and who had an actualised castration fantasy. After I became a training and supervising psychoanalyst, a younger colleague—let us call him Dr. Matlock—began receiving supervision from me while analysing a man named Smith. I was fascinated to learn that Smith's little finger was "accidentally" cut off just above the distal interphalangeal joint by his older brother on a camping trip. At that time he was eight and his brother was fourteen. Like Attis had done, Smith had placed his hand on a log being chopped by the older boy and the tip of his finger was lopped off. In addition to Smith and his brother being victims of this kind of physical trauma, both scenarios involved parents who could be grossly insensitive and unempathic with their offspring.

Smith, living on the East Coast of the United States, entered analysis with Dr. Matlock when he was fifty years old for panic and/or depressive states. Smith had never been married and from adolescence onwards was highly inhibited around women and men of authority. He suffered from premature ejaculation and erectile dysfunction, except when he was with a woman named Mary who lived on the West Coast of the United States. Although they lived over 2,000 miles apart, the two had been sexually involved for several decades. Smith would have an urgent impulse to fly and visit Mary again and again in spite of the fact that it was expensive and interfered with his routine work. He described his impulse to be with Mary not as a wish, but as a most puzzling *need*. Often Smith idealised her and called her a "perfect woman", despite much evidence that she was quite neurotic herself. After presenting aspects of Smith's life story I will present Smith's repeated visits to Mary as they reflect the influence of his actualised unconscious fantasy of being castrated.

Smith was the third of three sons born to his parents. His brothers were two and six years older respectively. He described his mother, an elementary school teacher, as a passive, waiflike woman who was utterly bereft of maternal qualities. She openly told him that she never loved his father and would have divorced him if it were not for him and his brothers. His father, a war veteran, worked as a foreman in a shipyard until his "conversion" in his late forties prompted him to resign this job and open a Christian bookstore. Smith described his father as a self-important man who disdained his sons, especially the two younger ones. Whenever his knowledge, opinions, or decisions were questioned he would fly into a rage. Smith thought his father an arrogant fool, although in his presence he never gave the slightest hint that he nurtured such a sentiment, he was so afraid of him.

Smith's middle brother was a reclusive child who spent much of his time in his room with his nose buried in books. A teacher once wrote a note to his mother in which she expressed her opinion that the child felt "neglected and unloved". His oldest brother was a sadistic boy who once tried to kill his middle brother by drowning him in a pool as Smith looked helplessly on. Had an adult not intervened to save the boy, he might have succeeded. The oldest brother, besides cutting off the tip of Smith's finger with an axe, also tried to sodomise Smith after he emerged from a shower several months later. When his parents were not around, this brother would taunt and tease Smith mercilessly. Sometimes these verbal assaults would turn physical and he would savagely beat his hapless brother.

Shortly after Smith's finger was cut off, his father noticed a swollen area near his son's groin during a bath. He was seen by a doctor who diagnosed a inguinal hernia about two inches from his penis. He received a hernial repair and remained in the hospital for several days to recuperate. Around this same time, his teacher decided that she would have her male students come to school dressed in girls' clothes. This terrified Smith; he went into "a tailspin of panic" and complained to the principal who cancelled this ill-conceived stunt. Dr. Matlock and I assumed that his difficulty going through a "normal" oedipal phase, having his finger cut off by his sadistic brother, being abused by the same brother, undergoing surgery, and being asked to dress like a girl combined to actualise Smith's castration anxiety.

At the pubertal age Smith was a shy, inhibited youngster, especially with girls. In high school it would often take him hours to find the courage to call a girl for a date. Upon graduation from high school, he attended college where he earned good marks and led a seemingly active social life, despite his shyness around young women. To manage his anxieties when in their company, he began to drink heavily and/or use drugs. He pledged a fraternity but resigned within a year because of the anxiety he felt around his fraternity brothers.

After college, he taught high school for a while and then decided to attend graduate school to work towards a master's degree in vocational counselling. His first job in his new career was as a vocational counsellor in a state mental hospital. He dreaded staff conferences where he had to present reports on patients he had evaluated because he would panic whenever he had to speak. In his analysis it would become clear that his motivation for working in a mental hospital included a wish to find solutions for his own psychological issues and/or project his difficulties onto others. Within a year he grew dissatisfied with this job and entered the military where he experienced his superiors as strong and stable parent figures. This helped him and eventually he was commissioned as an officer. After twenty years in the military he retired and started a business that he could manage mostly from his lonely home.

Smith sought psychoanalytic treatment soon after the death of his father. The father's death had rekindled aspects of unresolved oedipal issues which permeated the copious dream material that he brought to his sessions during the initial phase of his analysis. Typical of these dreams was one in which two planes (penises) were flying side by side. He compared the airplanes and then tried to shoot the other one down, experiencing anxiety while doing so. Both planes landed safely but as he deplaned the other pilot came after him and tried to kill him.

Now let me return to Smith's need to visit Mary, which had continued after he entered psychoanalysis. These visits sometimes interfered with his hold on his psychoanalytic appointments. Smith declared that he had no intention of marrying Marry, but he had to be with her, especially following an event that made him feel humiliated, such as when he faced a problem in his business or was treated badly by an older male waiter at a restaurant. He was well into the first year of his analysis when Dr. Matlock was informed, almost as an aside, about how Smith's trips to be with Mary were directly related to the actualisation of his castration fantasy. Upon his return from a weekend trip to the West Coast, Smith opened his session by saying, "We [meaning him and Mary] feed off each other. But what we really have most in common is our deformed little finger." It was then that Dr. Matlock and I learned that Mary too had lost part of a finger. Smith continued, "We are a couple of neurotics in love."

He described how, before having sex, he and Mary would place together their cut fingers as if one partial finger was an extension of the other partial finger. Then Smith would not have erectile dysfunction or premature ejaculation. Dr. Matlock silently formulated that two half fingers make a whole finger (whole penis) and that Smith, through a mental fusion of the two fingers, was undoing his actualised castration. This was why he needed to fly to the West Coast again and again. Later in Smith's analysis we were able to adduce more data supporting Dr. Matlock's formulation about the meaning of these trips.

For Smith, two cut fingers touching one another did not simply create a symbol of an uncastrated penis; they created a protosymbol (Werner & Kaplan, 1963), and Smith experienced possessing a complete penis. Even his repeated experiences in "finding" his uncastrated penis and not simply its symbol included distortion of reality. Smith, unlike Attis, did not have formed delusions and hallucinations. He was able to test the reality in his daily life. Even though he had a history of fearing being killed by his sadistic brother and, in his dreams, by figures symbolising this brother and/or his father, he did not have an impulse to murder someone. Smith had a higher personality organisation than Attis.

Before returning to Attis' case let me mention my circumcision when I was eight years old. In the culture of the Muslim environment where I grew up, circumcision of boys was carried out without anaesthesia, usually between the ages of four and eight. Because of many compensatory and counterphobic factors, such as verbal preparation, ceremonies, and gifts, this procedure would become something strongly needed by the ego, so much so that the lack of it might be severely traumatic (Öztürk & Volkan, 1971). My circumcision took place in a room of our rented house in Nicosia. I was surrounded by my father and his adult male friends and relatives. I sat on my paternal uncle's lap. He held my legs apart as a barber circumcised me and as someone put a Turkish delight in my mouth. Everyone in the room clapped their hands and congratulated me for becoming a "man". I went through this religious/cultural developmental passage without any complications.

Attis' loss of one of his fingers when he was four years old and his mother's peculiar way of dealing with this loss during his childhood, in fact, for decades, were central events that shaped Attis' personal psychological structure, especially his difficulty with reality testing. In his own way he, in action, informed me about this at the beginning of his initial three-month stay at the North Carolina Memorial Hospital. As I have already stated, he broke his three-week silence while meeting with me as an inpatient only after showing his fingers from under the blanket behind which he was hiding and then drawing them back. He then described his hallucination of snakes and his fear that they would be cut by a guillotine. For me, snakes were symbols for his penis, but for Attis they were more than symbols. When a guillotine cut a snake into two parts the snake *was* his penis; he was terrified. After the time he wiggled his fingers from behind the blanket, Attis always concealed the stump of his finger beneath his other hand, and it would be years before he could show it to me without anxiety.

A mother's role in distorting reality for a child can play a significant part in the child's holding on to psychotic behaviour, especially when this distortion prevents a child from taming typical unconscious fantasies, such as those linked with separation–individuation and oedipal issues. The main storyline of Attis' actualised unconscious fantasy could be read in the following way: "I am castrated by my brother, my mother's extension, but my castrated penis *is* alive. I cannot psychologically separate from my mother as long as she possesses my penis." Later, in his mind, his actualised castration by his mother was condensed with his fantasy of being castrated and sodomised by his father. Then, in another bizarre action, Attis' mother saved her husband's removed appendix, which forced her son to have further strange fantasies, one of which was the most obvious one: his idea of eating his father's appendix in the service of "reaching up" for an oedipal escape. For Attis, his finger and his father's appendix in bottles were not simply symbols; they were penises. After his mother's death when he took the bottled finger to his home and put it into a dresser drawer in the bedroom he was sharing with Gloria he still could not believe that he repossessed his cut penis. After his mother's death Gloria represented his mother even more, and his "mother" lived on. By killing Gloria Attis hoped to separate psychologically from his mother. It was this thought that made him a potential wife killer.

Unlike Smith, Attis did not have erectile dysfunction or premature ejaculation. But, as I gathered more information about him, I learned that his love making was rather mechanical in the service of discharging his sexual excitement. He did not share with Gloria that he sometimes turned into a frog and perceived her vagina as a walrus (*vagina dentata*). Just as he divided his penises into three and vaginas into two, his self-representation was also split, in fact, fragmented. In the next chapter I will examine such a self-representation before I describe my further work with the Methodist minister.

CHAPTER FIVE

Thoughts on personality organisations

According to the classical psychoanalytic view, only neurotic patients are analysable, but even some individuals whom Freud attempted to treat had more psychological problems than individuals with typical neurotic conditions. Since the early days of psychoanalysis, patients with many types of psychopathology have visited psychoanalysts' offices. Nevertheless, when I started my training in psychiatry, patients accepted for psychoanalytic treatment were selected very carefully. There would be a serious evaluation of a patient's suitability for undergoing psychoanalysis, especially with a beginner in the field. If the therapist was still in psychoanalytic training this evaluation had to be approved by the supervisor. Individuals with enough ego strength, those considered to have only neurotic problems, were selected to undergo psychoanalysis.

In 1953, a few years before I came to the United States, some well-known psychoanalysts began to notice that it was an illusion that psychoanalysts *only* treated neurotic individuals. Under the umbrella, which they named the "widening scope of psychoanalysis", they began to have a discussion on this topic (A. Freud, 1954; Jacobson, 1954; Stone, 1954, Weigert, 1954). Anna Freud said:

> If all the skill, knowledge and pioneering effort which was spent on widening the scope of application of psychoanalysis had been employed instead on intensifying and improving our technique in the original field, I cannot help but feel that, by now, we would find the treatment of the common neuroses child's play, instead of struggling with their technical problems as we have continued to do. How do analysts decide if they are given the choice between returning to health half a dozen young people with good prospects in life but disturbed in their enjoyment and efficiency by comparatively mild neuroses, or to devote the same time, trouble and effort to one single borderline case, who may or may not be saved from spending the rest of his life in an institution? Personally, I can feel the pull in both directions, perhaps with a bias toward the former task; as a body, the [American] Psychoanalytic Association has inclined in recent years toward the latter. (A. Freud, 1954, pp. 610–611)

Anna Freud's preference was not followed. As years passed, along with the decrease in old-type "suitable cases" rushing to undergo psychoanalysis, many individuals with conditions above and beyond neurotic problems began filling the psychoanalysts' and psychoanalytic therapists' offices. This meant that aspects of classical psychoanalytic technique, which were designed to treat neurotic patients, would not be applicable in the treatment of individuals who have other types of mental problems. As I gained more and more experience in working with patients, I gave up focusing on surface diagnostic terms that referred to this or that type of neurosis or psychosis and preoccupation with symptoms and signs of mental problems. Of course, such diagnostic terms and definitions of signs and symptoms usually provide initial significant information about an individual. Also, diagnoses according to *The Diagnostic and Statistical Manual of Mental Disorders* (*DSM*), published by the American Psychiatric Association, is required in situations such as when a clinician needs to meet requirements for insurance coverage. When evaluating an individual's mental condition and/or soon after starting to work with this individual, I began to ask myself, "What am I treating?" This question can be answered by going beyond putting the patient under a diagnostic category and referring to signs and symptoms. Making an "internal map" of the individual's psychic structure is necessary in order to better understand intrapsychic conflicts. For me, treatment meant modification in the patient's internal map. This modification should be observed clinically when the patient starts performing psychological tasks that she could not perform effectively earlier.

In 1963, as well as in 1969, Donald Winnicott, a paediatrician who became a psychoanalyst and introduced us to his version of object relations theory, "played" with diagrams and wrote papers about what he considered a "circle" representing a person. He wrote: "Inside the circle is collected all the interplay of forces and objects that constitute the inner reality of the individual at this moment of time" (Winnicott, 1963, p. 75). By 1969 he was telling us that "the individual" was a relatively modern concept. Until a few hundred years ago, he informed us, outside of a few exceptional "total individuals" (Winnicott, 1969, p. 222) everyone was unintegrated. Even in 1969, when he wrote again about a circle representing a person, he believed that the world was mainly composed of individuals who could not achieve integration and be a total unit. He noted that it is necessary to divide this circle by putting a line down its centre and stated that "there must always be war or potential war along the line in the centre, on either side of the line there become organized groupings of benign and persecutory elements" (pp. 222–223). He continued: "Idealists often speak as if there were such a thing as an individual with no line down the middle in the diagram of the person, where there is nothing but benign forces for use for good purposes" (p. 223). If we find a person who appears to be free of "bad" forces and objects, this simply means that the individual "is getting relief from a real or imagined or a provoked or delusional persecution" (pp. 223–224).

Many years after I read Winnicott's papers I too began to "play" with a circle that stands for a person in order to define three main types of internal maps, personality organisations. The first one is the high-level (neurotic) personality organisation. It is represented by Winnicott's circle with a line down its centre. The individual who possesses this type of internal map has a capacity to tolerate ambivalence, since opposite halves of the circle touch one another even though they are divided by a line. I consider this line not as a straight line but a segmented one in order to illustrate that persons who possess a high-level (neurotic) personality organisation have an integrated self-representation in spite of their experiencing ambivalence. The degree of tolerance for ambivalent feelings, thoughts and perceptions will be different from person to person. Such individuals perceive object images or representations realistically while experiencing varying degrees of ambivalence about them. Their reality testing is good and they own both sides of their mental conflicts. These individuals' primary defence mechanism is repression and their anxiety has a signalling function, heralding internal danger stemming from mental conflicts. The psychoanalytic structural theory that divides mind into id, ego, and superego is applicable in formulating such individuals' mental conflicts and describing the role of the superego in relation to ego functions and pressure from the id. Classical psychoanalytic technique was designed and evolved to be utilised for such individuals. Pre-oedipal problems that appear during the psychoanalytic treatment of persons with high-level personality organisation are mostly due to defensive regressions and fixations, and not due to ego deficiencies. Such patients work through them, become more directly pre-occupied with oedipal issues, develop oedipal transference neurosis and then resolve it. At the end of their successful analytic process they make some parts of the line in the middle of the circle more flexible or more pronounced according to their improved reality testing.

We also treat individuals who cannot be represented by a circle with a segmented line down its centre. These are individuals whose primary defence mechanism is splitting. The circle's opposite sides do not touch each other, or touch each other only in limited areas. Therefore, we need to draw a new circle that is composed of two parts with a *gap* between them. A circle with a gap between its opposite sides stands for my second internal map, the low-level personality organisation. Individuals with low-level personality organisation do not possess a fully integrated self-representation. Persons with narcissistic or borderline pathology fit into this category.

A person with narcissistic personality organisation defensively separates what became known in the psychoanalytic literature as the "grandiose self" (being number one) from a devalued "hungry self". To illustrate this we can draw the grandiose self bigger than the hungry self within the circle and put space between them. Or, we can imagine a pecan pie on a plate with a slice removed fully, or mostly, from the rest of the pie. Persons with borderline personality organisation split their libidinally invested half of the circle from the representation of their aggressively invested half of the circle. Or, we can imagine another pecan pie on a plate cut in the middle and separated fully or mostly into two halves. Object representations of individuals with narcissistic or borderline personality organisation are also unintegrated. They do not own both sides of their mental conflicts to one degree or another, except in limited areas where the opposite parts still touch one another. We cannot effectively explain their mental conflicts with structural theory mainly because they do not have fully developed superegos. Theoretically speaking, a fully developed superego is one in which identifications with both punitive and loving aspects of paternal (and other caregivers') representations are integrated as compromise-formation takes place. Again, theoretically speaking, a fully developed superego only exists in people with high-level (neurotic) personality organisation, and anyone whose personality organisation is below the high-level range does not have a fully developed superego. Therefore, in the old psychoanalytic literature when psychoanalysts attempted to explain the psychology of persons with a low-level internal map, they used terms such as "forerunners of the superego", "precursors of the superego", "archaic superego", "superego lacunae", "benign superego", and "punitive superego".

Patients with a low-level internal map possess object relations conflicts linked with ego deficiencies, such as deficiency in utilising integration of self- and/or object images with associated affects and repression of "unwanted" mental contents, to one degree or another. Object relations conflict refers to tensions concerning integrating or not integrating libidinally and aggressively loaded self- and object images within, or externalising them on to others and re-internalising them. As Theodore Dorpat (1976) stated, conflicts between being dependent and becoming independent—or between a desire to be close to an object (and its representation) and a desire to be distant—cannot be understood without applying a theory of object relations. Sometimes persons with low-level personality organisation present oedipal material. A closer look suggests that by presenting oedipal material, they try to "reach up" (Boyer, 1961, 1983; Volkan, 1976, 1997, 2010) in order to get away from their preoedipal object relation conflicts. The treatment technique for dealing with individuals with a low-level internal map is to help them to experience and work through, borrowing a term from Melanie Klein (1946, 1948), "crucial juncture" experiences: a patient's bringing together her opposite self- and object images with their associated affects so that she can begin to mend her internal world. Only after she accomplishes such mending will the patient be capable of genuinely working through her oedipal issues with an integrated self-representation.

In order to visualise the third type of internal map, the psychotic personality organisation, consider hitting on the inside of Winnicott's circle with a hammer and smashing it into some big and many small pieces. The self-representation of persons with psychotic personality organisation is fragmented. Their object representations too are fragmented. Such individuals utilise fragmentation as their main mental defence system. They present primitive object relations conflicts accompanied with defects in ego functions, such as reality testing function. Fragmented self- and object images sometimes fuse and then diffuse, or are involved in an exaggerated and easily observable internalisation–externalisation cycle. For example, during a therapeutic hour the patient moves his mouth "eating" the analyst and then he externalises him by spitting. In chronic psychotic states the patient can hold on to one fragmented part or a very small number of sections and wipe out others with severe breaks with reality supported by established delusions and hallucinations. In such situations the internalisation–externalisation cycle cannot be easily observed.

Individuals who have *multiple personality organisation* (Brenner, 2001, 2004) exhibit an advanced version of psychotic personality organisation. Their fragmented self-images and corresponding object images have evolved to possess distinct characteristics and become stable enough for the individual to sense them, as if various identities (personalities) exist within the individual. The person usually gives them names—one is Madeline, the other one Grace, and still another one Fatima. One of these personalities, if advanced enough, does not recognise the lower-level ones since the function of repression is available to it. Meanwhile, the lower-level personalities, without the benefit of repression, may be aware of the existence of the highest one and sometimes each other.

The internalisation–externalisation cycle in individuals with a psychotic personality organisation is accompanied by a projection-introjections cycle. I use the terms *internalisation* and *externalisation* to describe the in and out movements of self- and object images, and the terms *introjection* and *projection* to refer to sending thoughts, affects, perceptions, and protosymbols (Werner & Kaplan, 1963) inward or outward, often resulting in a sense of internal destruction or paranoid expectation. Persons with the third kind of internal map show no sophisticated "fit" between what is internalised/introjected, and the reality of the object or thing before it is taken in, and no sophisticated "fit" between what is externalised/projected and the target. Furthermore, the internalisation–externalisation cycle in such individuals is not masked by sophisticated symbols. Patients with psychotic personality organisation do not experience typical anxiety that has a signalling function for sensing a mental conflict. Anxiety can evolve as an "emotional flooding" (Volkan, 1976) and become overwhelming for the patient. Such individuals defend themselves from experiencing emotional flooding by further fragmentation and further fusion-diffusion, externalisation-internalisation, projection-introjection cycles, and/or wiping out more reality.

Patients with psychotic personality organisation too sometimes utilise "reaching up" (Boyer, 1961, 1983; Volkan, 1976, 1997, 2010): they bring up oedipal material, typically in an unmasked (unrepressed) fashion, in order to escape their primitive object relations conflicts. Approaching such individuals with classical psychoanalytic technique will go nowhere. The useful technique for them will first aim to help them develop a new healthy mental core that will support the individual to move up to a low-level personality organisation. There are cases with of people with psychotic personality organisation who, by going through psychoanalytic treatment, reach a high-level personality organisation. My description of the treatment of Jane, from its beginning to its end (Volkan, 1995), is such an example. Later in this book I will present an overview of the treatment process of Ricky, who was also able to change his psychotic internal map and, through psychoanalytic therapy, to reach a high-level personality organisation. This book will also describe how the Methodist minister changed his internal map.

The interplay between age-appropriate experiences and the maturation of the central nervous system, the importance of a "fit" between the infant and the mother in the development of what psychoanalysts call "ego functions", and ability to form mental images of relationships with others ("object relations") have been scientifically studied, especially since the 1970s (for example, see: Greenspan, 1997, 1989; Stern, 1985; Emde, 1991; Brazelton & Greenspan, 2000; Purhonen, Pääkkönen, Yppärilä, Lehtonen & Karhu, 2001; Lehtonen, 2003; Bloom, 2010). One fact we learned is that an infant's mind is more active than we had thought decades ago when we used to speak about an "autistic phase" (Mahler, 1968). But, no matter how much potential and ability an infant possesses, in infancy no one has a fully separate self; the infant's mind can be conceptualised as being in a creative state of confusion. From René Spitz's work (1946, 1965) decades ago on smiling response, separation anxiety, and stranger anxiety, to John Bowlby's (1953, 1969) examination of attachment, to Henri Parens' (2007) more recent studies, we have learned how the child slowly develops the ability to differentiate herself from others and also to differentiate between various internalised or external object images. The child also develops an integrating ego function that allows her to put together, mend, previously separated opposite self- and or object images. As Daniel Stern (1985) noted, an infant is fed four to six times a day and each feeding experience produces different degrees of pleasure. Stern illustrates that as the child grows up, different experiences become categorised in the child's mind as "good" and "bad" (see also Lehtonen's 2003 studies). We hear *echoes* of Harry Stack Sullivan's (1962) description of "good me", "bad me", "good mother", "bad mother", and "not me", and writings of others on the type of object relation theory that concerns the internalisation of interpersonal experiences that remain inside the individual's mental structure (Jacobson, 1964; Kernberg, 1966, 1975, 1976, 1980, 1988; Volkan, 1976, 1995; Dorpat, 1976; Gedo, 1979). This type of object relations theory stresses the formation of self- and object images and representations contaminated with affects that reflect the original infant–mother relationship as well as the subsequent development of more mature dyadic, triadic, and multiple internal and external relations with more differentiated affects in general. Only after the development of integrative ego function in the service of integrating opposites does a child evolve the concept and sense of being "average" and tolerance of ambivalence.

I emphasised the differentiation and integration of ego functions when defining the three types of internal maps. When a person has a high-level (neurotic) personality organisation he is capable of utilising both differentiation and integration functions. When an adult has low-level personality organisation he is capable of differentiation, but not capable of integration to one degree or another. In his case the "normal splitting" that we see during a small child's mental development does not disappear for all practical purposes, but turns into "defensive splitting" and then is utilised as the main mental defence in adulthood. When a person has a psychotic personality organisation, both his differentiation and integration functions are deficient. An adult with a psychotic internal map turns this deficiency into defensive utilisation and holds on to fragmentation, fusion/diffusion, and internalisation-externalisation as primary mental defences.

In practice, it is sometimes difficult to make very clear distinctions between the three types of personality organisations. Even a person who has fragmented self- and object images can behave for some short or long time as a person with a higher level personality organisation. This occurs when this person can hold onto a self-image that is rather advanced without including it in speedy fusion-diffusion or internalisation–externalisation cycles. Attis could hold on to his Methodist minister self-concept and behave, at least on the surface, as a "normal" individual for short or long periods of time. I suggest that thinking of three types of internal maps can serve as a guide for the therapist as to how to begin and continue treating a patient.

CHAPTER SIX

The psychotic core

Since Attis is the main subject of this book I will continue to play with the internal map of a psychotic personality organisation. I will place a metaphorical doughnut in the middle of the fragmented circle belonging to such an individual. This metaphorical doughnut represents the *psychotic core*, which in my earlier writings I named "infantile psychotic self" (Volkan, 1995) or "the seed of madness" (Volkan & Akhtar, 1997). My metaphorical doughnut is a filled doughnut, filled with rotten jelly, distasteful affects as expression of aggression.

Psychoanalytic theories on aggression go all the way back to Freud's inconsistent thoughts on this topic prior to his coming up with the "death instinct" in 1920 (Freud, 1920g), an idea out of favour in today's psychoanalytic literature. Today there are considerations that fit Henri Parens' (1979 [2008]) "multi-trends theory of aggression". Parens states that the way parents rear their child is a direct factor in that child's aggression profile, while he also considers the role of a child's average-expectable biological conditions in this profile. The quality of attachment and the child's aggression profile are linked. Parens describes a wide range of affective expressions, from anger to hostility, to rage, to hate, to benign or malignant prejudice. Adults with a psychotic internal map sometimes present such affective expressions. However, the affective expressions in the middle of my metaphorical doughnut, which develop in childhood, are unnameable, or they can only be described as "excessive unpleasure" (Kernberg, 1966).

When I was working intensively with numerous individuals with psychotic personality organisation, some of them spontaneously described the existence of a "doughnut" in their internal worlds. Attis never used this analogy. Those who actually used the word "dough-nut" seemed to be referring to a ring doughnut with the dough missing in the middle. For them, the missing middle stood for an "emptiness" they felt in the core of their mental existence. They, in fact, did not have ring doughnuts, but filled doughnuts. However, by utilising extensive denial, they managed to perceive the rotten jelly as "noth-ing", and hold on to an illusion that unbearable unpleasantness/ aggression was erased. I agree with Peter Fonagy and Mary Target (Fonagy & Target, 2002) that a patient's feeling "empty" and denying her existence by generalising this feeling can also be in the service of protecting herself from being attacked and "killed" by another person perceived as a dangerous bad object. People do not kill you if you do not exist. The patient, as Fonagy and Target stated, may also empty the other person in order that that person is not a target of her mur-derous aggression.

Let us re-visualise the filled doughnut in the middle of the smashed circle. Its inside looks like a sponge soaked with rotten jelly. The sponge is surrounded by fragmented self- and internalised object images. The rotten jelly oozes into gaps between fragmented images. It is the rotten jelly that prevents the pieces of the self- and internalised object images from getting together and mending. Such patients, in fact, are preoc-cupied with attempts to change the "bad" jelly to "good" jelly. They are "object addicts" (Fenichel, 1945, p. 436); they need to find ways for libidinal objects to be internalised. Donald Burnham (1969) wrote about the individual with my third-type internal map and stated:

> The very excessiveness of his need for objects also makes them inordinately dangerous and fearsome since they can destroy him through abandonment ... They can make or break him ... Thus threat may be further understood if we consider that his precari-ously balanced inner structure is extraordinarily vulnerable to external influences in its most literal sense, "flowing into". He lacks adequate insulation from others ... Like a ship at sea without

adequate navigational equipment, he requires directions from external sources. (Burnham, 1969, p. 28)

The aim of a psychoanalytically informed treatment of people who possess such a condition is to replace the rotten jelly with a sweet (libidinal) one that will function as a glue for mending fragmented elements.

Today, the dominant tendency for explaining why someone suffers from schizophrenia or has psychotic signs and symptoms is to present data from ongoing extensive research on brain functions, micro-injuries, neurodevelopmental alterations, and genetics. I am not an expert in examining fully and evaluating findings from such research. I have studied some of those that have general relevance for psychoanalysis (for example: Reiser, 1990; Tienari, 1991; Leigh & Reiser, 1992; Van der Kolk, 2000; Beutel, Stern & Silbersweig, 2003; Levin, 2004; Solms & Turnbull, 2010 & Laufer, 2013). Robert Cancro's statement years ago that biological theories are "devoid of psychological content" and "increasingly suffer from reductionism" (Cancro, 1986, p. 106) remains true. Cancro also wrote: "Theory can only be useful within a particular realm of discourse, and psychoanalytic theory must function within its assumptions it utilizes" (Cancro, 1986, p. 106). He hoped that in the future our understanding of the biology of mental activities such as memory and thought would become rich enough to help us shift from the universe of psychology into that of biology with ease. He imagined that when this happened it might be possible to include biological concepts in psychoanalytic theories.

During a child's developmental years, genetic and neurological factors can become combined with psychological ones in the creation of a psychotic core saturated with unnameable "bad/aggressive" affects. Also, let us not forget familial, cultural, religious influences, and the impact of wars and warlike conditions on a child's developing internal world. We also have information that illustrates that when the psychology of a person changes, due to psychotherapy for example, biological changes in the brain also occur. The problem here is this: when an adult with a third-type internal map, psychotic personality organisation, comes for psychotherapy, the clinician usually does not know or cannot evaluate the exact mixture of biological factors with psychological ones and what the most influential factors are for the patient's existing condition. Certainly, some patients who exhibit psychotic symptoms do have neurological deficits. Can other patients' psychotic symptoms be due *only* to psychological factors? My answer is "yes". My experience with Attis, more of which will be described later, is one reason I give this answer. While certain neurological or genetic alterations can be measured and examined in typical scientific ways, I cannot imagine a typical scientific way to study and measure an *unconscious* fantasy as I described earlier in this book and its role in shaping someone's internal map.

My personal work for decades with individuals like Attis, and my observations during three months per year for the last ten years at the Austen Riggs Center in Stockbridge, Massachusetts, have taught me a great deal about multiple *psychological* factors that play a key role in establishing a psychotic core in a developing child. At the Austen Riggs Center, twice weekly case presentations include extensive reports on these cases' family backgrounds, often including their ancestors' history. We need to go beyond Frieda Fromm-Reichmann's (1959) old "schizophregenic mother" image and be more *specific* about how the child's mother as well as other mothering persons function in relation to the child. Some mothers and/or family members cannot provide a reasonable "fit" between their own activities and temperaments and those of their children. Children being presented with mental functions that create "unassimilable contradiction" (Burnham, 1969, p. 55) have been studied (for example, see: Torsti, 1998; Alanen, 1993; Greenspan, 1997; Brazelton & Greenspan, 2000; Tizón, 2007). How a parent's inability to think about the child's mental experiences deprive the child of the chance to form a viable sense of himself has also been examined extensively (Fonagy & Target, 1997). Sometimes, important individuals in the child's environment interfere with the child's transitional object (Winnicott, 1953). This interferes with the child's working through his "experiments" to separate mother-me from external objects. I frequently noted cases when the mother or mothering person interfered with the child's reality testing, integrative function, and developing a body image. Such interferences occurred in Attis' case.

Now I will focus on mothering persons' and the child's specific type of unconscious fantasies, interactions between them, and their role in a child's holding on to a primitive internal map with a doughnut in its middle filled with rotten jelly. Maurice Apprey (1997) and Gabriele Ast and I (Volkan & Ast, 1997) describe some mothers' unconscious fantasy that their children disappear or die. A child's own unconscious fantasy corresponding to her mother's unconscious fantasy, when it is put into words, could be read in the following way: "My mother did not wish me to be born. I should get rid of my (mental) self and have a psychological death in order to please my mother and thus turn her into the longed-for 'good' mother." Such an unconscious fantasy, especially when it is actualised, can stop the child's mental development to one degree or another and make the child hold on to "bad" affects and thus develop a psychotic core. Committing oneself to a psychological death goes along with the maintenance of "excessive unpleasure".

A patient's initial family history and initial signs and symptoms can suggest clues about the existence of a mother's or mothering person's death wish for a child and the child's corresponding unconscious fantasy. For example, a person with psychotic personality organisation presented a family story in which the patient was conceived a week prior to the mother's planned surgery to have her tubes tied. In another case, there was a family scenario in which the mother did not know that she was pregnant until the seventh month of her pregnancy. Both patients had repeating dreams of disappearing and sometimes reappearing as a symbolic baby in another environment, and delusions of having other parents or, in the second case, also being brought to Earth from outer space. The second patient tried to change her name and carved a new name on her body.

Besides a mother's or mothering person's unconscious fantasy that her child disappears, and the child's corresponding actualised unconscious fantasy, there are other unconscious fantasies in the dyadic relationship that play a role in the child's establishing and holding on to a psychotic core. Frances, in her mid-twenties, had a psychotic personality organisation. Before she became my patient she had communicated with spirits and allowed a religious cult leader to perform an exorcism on her to remove the "devil" in her chest, her psychotic core. She was adopted as a newborn baby primarily to replace her adoptive mother's brother, a pilot who had lost his life after an accident just prior to the adoption. Frances' adoptive maternal grandmother, who performed most of the mothering functions for Frances, openly talked about God taking away her son and then giving Frances to the family. The grandmother often referred to Frances as a reincarnation of Francis, the dead pilot (Volkan & Ast, 1997). As a child, Frances was given the dead pilots' childhood toys to play with. The mother and the grandmother had both conscious and unconscious fantasies that the child they adopted was also the dead pilot. Frances, as a "living linking object" (Volkan, 1981a), as a "replacement child" (Cain & Cain, 1964; Legg & Sherick, 1976; Green & Solnit, 1964; Poznanski, 1972; Ainslie & Solyom, 1986; Volkan & Ast, 1997), had an unconscious fantasy of being a reincarnated individual. Frances' developmental push to find herself and individuate, and the force stemming from her mother's and grandmother's shared unconscious fantasy to keep her as an extension of a dead person, along with her corresponding unconscious fantasy of containing a reincarnated man in her self-representation, created psychic confusion, unnameable bad affects as a rotten jelly inside her, and triggered her to form a psychotic core.

Here is still another factor forcing a child to develop and maintain a seed of madness. The child's experiencing a drastic actual trauma or series of actual traumas and suffering from mental torture—ranging from being a subject for actual torture by a sibling to being sexually abused by a priest or uncle—can cause the evolution of a psychotic core. Severe regressions occurring after adolescence and the second individuation (Blos, 1979) due to severe traumas will not produce a psychotic core (Volkan, 1997). Persons exposed to such post-adolescence severe traumas may exhibit defensive regressive fixations and aggressive behaviour but they do not develop a filled doughnut that contains rotten jelly. I agree with Thomas Freeman (1983) that we should not perceive psychosis as a regressed extension of neurosis. True psychosis develops after one goes through the adolescence passage and in adulthood because of the existence of a childhood psychotic core, even if it may have been previously hidden.

I have illustrated different fates of the psychotic core in my previous writings (Volkan, 1997). According to the type of fate, the surface manifestations will also appear in different ways. If the bad jelly in childhood floods profusely into the rest of the circle that represents the child, she develops a clinical picture of childhood psychosis. If the flooding is not profuse, the child may appear "normal" in certain ways, but since the rotten jelly oozes out of the encapsulating dough she will also exhibit some bizarre signs and symptoms to one degree or the other, such as screaming. In adulthood too, when the doughnut functions like an effective sponge, absorbing most of the rotten jelly so that only parts of the remaining fragmented self- and internalised object images are contaminated, the patient exhibits "normal" behaviour to one degree or another. However, she is also exhibits bizarre behaviours, separated from her "normal" activities. Bizarre behaviour activities are directly related to ego defences against sensing the impact of the bad jelly absorbed by the dough. For example, I supervised for years the psychoanalytic psychotherapy of a young woman who was an intelligent person, a graduate of a well-known law school. She was married and in many ways she was a good wife. Since her husband was very rich she did not work. At home she had dozens and dozens of cats. The unusual thing about this "hobby" was the fact that these cats had leukaemia; she would take care of only sick cats and spent a great deal of her time with veterinarians. In her daily life her reality testing was good; for example when she purchased things at a grocery store she knew that she had to pay for her purchased items with a smile on her face. During her treatment her therapist and I slowly became keenly aware that her sick cats represented her psychotic core. It was externalised into the cats and they had to be under constant care. Her other bizarre symptom told us more about how these cats actually were part of her core. She had undergone six reconstructive operations in a conscious attempt to make her face resemble that of a cat.

If the contamination of the diagram of the person with rotten jelly is generalised, the adult who has this condition may perceive himself as a "monster" or use another term descriptive of being filled with unpleasant unnameable aggressive affects. He may also feel "empty", as I have already described, when the existence of the monster is completely denied. In some cases, the patient refers to an internalised object image that becomes soaked with unnameable aggression and, for example, calls himself "Jack the Ripper". The patient does so with a hope that no other "bad" object can come close to him to provide more rotten jelly for his psychotic core. In cases when the patient develops a defensive illusion of internalising a "good" libidinal image and maintaining it within himself he can also become an "angel". A patient can cling to one type of existence or non-existence for days or even months. Often, being Jack the Ripper or an angel can alternate quickly or slowly due to the patient's internalisation–externalisation cycle.

Sometimes, usually in the teen years or in early adulthood, a specific trauma, usually one that unconsciously reminds the individual of a primary trauma of his childhood or a dysfunctional childhood attachment issue, squeezes the metaphorical doughnut, even though earlier he was to a great extent able to contain the bad jelly. The rotten jelly quickly erupts through its container with force and fills up the rest of the self- and object images in the circle. The patient experiences not anxiety, but an "emotional flooding" (Volkan, 1974, 1976, 1981b, 1995) or "organismic panic" (Pao, 1979). He also develops what classical analysts called "world destruction fantasies" (Fenichel, 1945). Such a clinical picture describes an acute episode of a schizophrenic condition. I believe that James Glass' (1985) study at the Sheppard and Enoch Pratt Hospital of the psychological breakdown of the inner world of adults entering acute schizophrenia is a classic. Glass describes, for example, patients feeling that a star is exploding into millions of pieces within them. Later world destruction fantasies will alternate with "world construction fantasies" (Fenichel, 1945) also associated in bizarre ways with disturbances in reality testing, delusion, and hallucinations. Nowadays, quickly medicating patients is robbing us of the opportunity to notice these processes.

Attis dealt with his seed of madness from early childhood onwards. In his adulthood many psychiatrists diagnosed him as suffering from schizophrenia. He was also given the same diagnosis at the North Carolina Memorial Hospital. Only later would I, during my clinical work, be uninterested, or less interested, in making a surface diagnosis according to a person's signs and symptoms, instead focusing on the person's internal map and the fate of the psychotic core.

Now I will return to my relationship with Attis. Starting in the next chapter I illustrate how he would slowly make changes to his internal doughnut with its "bad" jelly.

CHAPTER SEVEN

Beginning outpatient therapy

When I began working with Attis I did not know the concepts I described in the previous three chapters, although my inpatient supervisor and, after Attis was discharged from the hospital, my outpatient supervisor had had psychotherapeutic involvement with patients like him. If I had been an experienced clinician at that time and if Attis could have driven to Chapel Hill more than once a week after his discharge from his hospitalisation, the therapeutic process that would have evolved between us would have obviously taken a different course. Notes that I kept after each meeting with my outpatient supervisor reflect my bewilderment as well as excitement.

When Attis was an inpatient I met him in his hospital room for his therapy sessions, a secure environment for him and for me. Now and then I would also greet him briefly when I visited the unit to meet with my other patients or to speak with the nurses and other personnel. Experienced nurses were available to look after him twenty-four hours a day. Following his discharge from hospital it was only the two of us, starting a new journey together in one of the rather small rooms at North Carolina Memorial Hospital's psychiatric outpatient services facility. I would learn much later about how a therapist's room, its appearance and items within it, become symbolic extensions of a psychoanalyst, and how any changes in the room become involved in transference–countertransference issues (Volkan, 2010). For example, one of my patients once noticed that I had forgotten to water a potted plant and this induced her recollections of being deprived of her mother's love. Gable, to whom I have referred briefly, saw a postcard on my table during the second year of his analysis that had been sent to me from Turkey illustrating two half-naked men wrestling at a traditional wrestling competition. This led to further opening of his oedipal fears by sexualising our relationship in the transference. When I started to see Attis as an outpatient, the hospital's psychiatric services only offered psychiatric residents their choice of small rooms with only two chairs and an empty desk. When Attis was present I would see him in whichever of these rooms was available; we could not even meet in the same place for each of our sessions, and frequently meeting in different rooms supported his fragmentation of my image as well as his.

As mentioned earlier, Anna Freud (1968) noted that patients with high-level (neurotic) personality organisation enter psychoanalysis (or psychotherapy) with an attitude towards the psychoanalyst that is largely based on reality, and only later, within the context of a deepening treatment, develops a full-blown transference that becomes a transference neurosis. She explains: "To the extent to which a person [with the first type of internal map] has a healthy part of his personality, his real relationship to the analyst is never wholly submerged" (A. Freud, 1968, p. 373). A patient with a high-level personality organisation in ordinary transference activates aspects of an infantile and/or early childhood self, and aspects of parenting and other childhood object images. With therapeutic work, activated aspects of the infant's or small child's self-images are linked to and integrated with the patient's self-representation. Activated aspects of parenting and other object images are, in turn, linked to or integrated with the parenting figure and other representations as experienced in infancy and early childhood (Kernberg, 1976). Such linking and integration of what is activated with the rest of the self- and object representations do not occur in the transference manifestations of a person with Attis' internal map. From the beginning of the therapeutic relationship, a patient with a psychotic personality organisation will involve the therapist's and her own various corresponding images in her fusion-diffusion and externalisation-internalisation, accompanied with projection-introjection cycles in an unrealistic fashion in very open or hidden, and fast or slow, ways.

I still remember Attis' very first outpatient session with me. He sat in front of me tightly holding the arms of his chair while managing to hide his cut finger. He appeared poised to experience a deadly earthquake. For fifty minutes he insisted that he was a "monster". Thanks to the support of my outpatient supervisor, I was well prepared. I tried to stay calm and spoke now and then, making remarks about our starting a "new trip" together. I explained that there was no need for us to be in a hurry. After my first session with Attis as an outpatient my new supervisor explained to me that Attis internalised aggressively loaded images and kept them within himself, attempting to become a scary "monster" during his session in order to protect himself from me because he had externalised more severely loaded aggressive self- and object images onto me. I found it very useful that my first and second supervisors were saying the same thing in relation to their approach to my patient. Attis continued to remain a "monster" during the following sessions.

Around the time Attis started his weekly outpatient treatment with me, I accomplished a major milestone in my adjustment to life in the United States: I bought an old used car and learned how to drive it. During my first year of residency my monthly salary, as I recall now, was seventy-five dollars. I also received free meals at the hospital on working days. I cannot say exactly how seventy-five dollars in the early 1960s corresponds to that amount today, but I am sure it would not amount to a reasonable level for a young physician. I learned how to pay for the old car through instalments. Unlike my experience in Chicago where I was surrounded by medical interns and residents who were all foreigners like me, in Chapel Hill all my fellow psychiatry residents were Americans. I imagined their salaries were identical with mine. Unlike me, as I understood, some of them were borrowing money from banks with the knowledge that they would be able to pay their debts once they finished their residency and started their professional life. As a foreigner I could not do this. (At that time I had not yet planned to stay in the United States after my training in psychiatry and become an American citizen.) When I was living in Cyprus my family could not afford a car and I had not learned how to drive. A fellow psychiatry resident in Chapel Hill, David Fuller, who now resides in Texas, kindly gave me driving lessons. I bet David never realised how important his "gift" was for me: I could join other psychiatry residents' social gatherings and expand my horizons to learn the American way of life as it existed in a small university town. Looking back, I wonder now if, as a foreigner, I had identified with Attis. He was "isolated" because of his psychotic core, and I was "isolated" because I did not know how to drive a car. If I could do something about my "isolation", he could, when the time came, identify with my ability to expand one's horizons.

Whenever Attis visited me Gloria accompanied him to Chapel Hill and met with Rebecca. One day I saw Attis and Gloria in the hospital's parking lot when they were getting out of their car. In comparison to my old car they had a shiny new one. I believe that I did not feel jealousy. This is because, while growing up in Cyprus a car was not a symbol for manhood for me. My family could afford to buy me a bicycle and I could compare my bicycle with bicycles of other youngsters in my neighbourhood. Owning a bicycle was my childhood symbol of attaining status as a young man. I still recall with great fondness waking up one morning in my early teen years and noticing a brand new bicycle next to my bed. My parents had bought it for me and put it in my bedroom after I fell asleep so I would be surprised the next morning.

The Methodist Church took good care of Attis. I learned from the social worker that, not only did the Church make sure that he drove a shiny new car, they also sent people to gently check on him and protect Gloria. I also learned that Attis had started to carry out his duties at the church soon after his discharge from hospital. According to Gloria, people in general had heard the "rumour" that he had tried to kill his wife, but those who attended the church services were supportive by going along with Gloria's declaration that conducting too many funeral services was the cause of Attis' distress. As far as I could learn, Attis was capable of rendering the routine church services. In his sessions with me he would not talk about his daily life. My supervisor suggested that Attis bringing his psychotic transference onto me by presenting himself as "monster", while in fact in a hidden way protecting himself from me—a more vicious "monster"—due to his externalisations and projections, was helping Attis to remain "normal" in his rural environment. He encouraged me to continue to tolerate this bizarre behaviour. A person with a high-level personality organisation brings transference manifestations to sessions. But the analyst waits—unless such manifestations become a source of obstacle for therapeutic work—until the patient evolves a *workable* transference neurosis to work on it with the patient. Similarly, transference psychosis manifestations that a patient with a psychotic core exhibits at the beginning of his treatment are not entry points for therapeutic progress until the patient develops a workable transference psychosis. Later, I will share with the reader the evolution of Attis' workable transference psychosis and how, through our working through it, he made significant progress in changing his internal world.

As some months passed by I noticed that when Attis and I met in a therapy room he no longer grabbed the arms of the chair while sitting in front of me. One day he hallucinated his father's face on the wall in the therapy room. At that time Attis himself was not a "monster". I suspected that I was also not a "hidden monster". A terrifying object image, his father's face, was externalised on a wall. He began pouring out references to other terrifying objects "out there," such as his wife's walrus/vagina and a "bitch", a female parishioner whom he disliked and who stood for his "bad" mother/the fortune teller in the rural area where he was born. I noticed that he felt more comfortable with me; both of us now could "watch" together his externalised "bad" images separate from both of us, such as on the wall. Even though I could not actually see his father's face, I could regress enough in the service of joining Attis to sense its existence.

When Attis continued to repeat similar scenarios in his following sessions, this time externalising his terrifying object image more directly onto Gloria, I wished to help him change his external target, since I wanted him to be more comfortable at home. Looking back, perhaps I was afraid that he might become homicidal again. I have no references about such a consideration in my old notes. In any case, without using technical words, I would tell him how he might be displacing his dead mother/the "bitch" image onto his wife. Then, as if he were imitating me, he would repeat my exact statement. It was as if he would "eat" my statement, but without assimilating it, he would then spit it out. My remarks would not make him curious, or defensive, or grateful as a person with the first kind of internal map might. But, I also felt that his sensing that I "knew" what was bothering him was supportive to him.

Within a few months I had a drastic experience with Attis "reaching up" (Boyer, 1971, 1983). During his therapy sessions, Attis talked openly about incestuous wishes and other aspects of oedipal striving. His abundant production of bizarre fantasies of having sex with his mother and identifying with his sadistic father (as when his father would put a stick up a donkey's anus) seemed like a kind of primitive obsessional defence. However, he was far from being considered a person suffering from an obsessional neurosis. He was simply "reaching up". His obsession with oedipal issues, which was not accompanied by the benefit of repression, was in the service of his attempts to control object relations conflicts and eruptions of rather raw emotions.

My supervisor suggested that I only listen to this material without blaming Attis. This, I did. Later in my career I would read and learn more about how it is a mistake for the therapist faced with a patient like Attis to regard oedipal material as something to deal with, as if the patient were functioning at the oedipal level. I concur with Rosenfeld (1965) and Boyer (1971, 1983) in their belief that interpretation of such oedipal material on a libidinal level, when it is offered to this kind of patient, can promote psychotic excitement; the patient can all too readily see in such interpretation a seductive invitation on the part of the therapist. Boyer (1971) states:

> If I refer to such material, I do so from the standpoint of its aggressive and manipulative aspects or interpret upwards ... Thus, as an example, if the patient relates that he has open fantasies of intercourse with his mother, I respond that he must love her very much. I believe that the patient who suffers from a severe characterological or schizophrenic disorder has massive fears of the vicissitudes of his aggressive impulses and that analysis proceeds smoothest when attention is directed gently but consistently towards the analysis of the protective manoeuvres he employs to defend against his fear that his hostility will result in the analyst's death or his own. (p. 70)

Attis confessed that during this time he was sexually dysfunctional with Gloria because of incestuous implications, and fear of retaliation from his father's representation and what I might do to him. I told him openly that I would not hurt him and that I was more interested in being curious about what had made him busy with sexualised images of his parents. I did not tell him that he "loved" his mother, but suggested that his sexualised fantasies about his mother might be a search for a loving mother. I also shared with him my observation that he reached towards sexualised material after he had been preoccupied with scary objects such as his father's face on the wall, the "bitch", and his wife's vagina. I added that when he started to tell me about sexual wishes he ended up once more facing danger, as if there was no way to feel secure. I wanted him to know that his dangerous perceptions might have something to do with his childhood experiences, such as his finding himself in a burning house or hearing a neighbour harming his own body. I did not give more details, but stated that we would go at his pace to understand his fears. He calmed down.

About six months after he started his outpatient therapy with me, I learned that Gloria would attend a teachers' conference in a neighbouring state that was important for her career. As her departure approached, Attis' terror increased once more. I noticed that he also increased his fusion of his wife's mental representation with that of his rejecting mother image while his thoughts of murdering her in order to find his "freedom" also reappeared. I understood that he could no longer function at church.

I told Attis how an external event—Gloria's expected departure— was creating severe difficulties in his internal world and because of this I wanted to re-hospitalise him. Referring to the reappearance of his murderous thoughts about Gloria, I explained to him that if he did something aggressive and was put in a prison I would not know how to maintain our therapeutic relationship since he would not then be able come to see me regularly. By then I had learned the English phrase, "It takes two to tango" and I used it to emphasise that our work needed two persons—he and I—since my dancing alone while he was in prison would take neither of us anywhere. Therefore, I was asking him to stay in the hospital before Gloria's departure and for a while after her return until the impact of this event settled down. I remember how he smiled and agreed to come back to the hospital. He felt comfortable there, appeared "normal", and on several occasions told nurses that he was back because he was, at this time in his life, sensitive about "losing" Gloria, since he had not yet fully mourned his mother's death.

In addition to the time just before Gloria's departure and while she was away for a week or so, Attis remained in the hospital one more month. One reason for this was the church authorities' decision not to return Attis to his church. Apparently, Baptist Pastor Johns was spreading more and more vicious rumours about Attis because of his re-hospitalisation. The church authorities gave Attis a leave of absence. He and his wife moved to a new rural area over 100 miles away from the previous location and now 150 miles away from Chapel Hill. He became the Methodist minister of a smaller church. I learned that this area was a beautiful place and near a resort area with golf courses and swimming pools.

As Attis was settling into this new place, he attended all his weekly sessions with me. Now, I was observing in a more concrete fashion another version of transference psychosis. Instead of remaining as a "monster", he "fused" with my protective image. In a metaphorical sense, I was located in his internal doughnut absorbing the rotten jelly, and keeping it from flooding the rest of his self-representation. He therefore became concerned about my health and welfare. I would tell him that I was alright, and able to keep my mental capacities. In those days at work we always wore ties while seeing patients. One day I noticed that Attis had purchased a tie exactly like mine and he was wearing it. Two men wearing the same tie were meeting in a small therapy room. Soon this situation became even more interesting. Attis began to dress like me, becoming like me, and telling me, using my own words, that he was alright and that he could keep his mental functions and work as a minister. He would tell me about his sermons at the church and I would notice his repetition of some sentence that I had uttered a week before during our sessions, such as, "We do not need to hurry," or, "I tell you, curiosity will not kill us or damage us."

I began learning a great deal about the childhood stories already reported earlier in this book. Sometimes he could even "intellectually" connect these stories with events in his adult life. I did not "interpret" his identification with me. My supervisor and I wondered if his keeping my "good" image in his psychotic core would continue. Would he be able to assimilate my image effectively? We doubted that this "identification" with me would settle in him. However, it was good to see such a process; when the time came, he could repeat it with a more permanent outcome.

In general, after moving to his new location and bein physically away from Pastor Johns, Attis' terror seemed much tamer, and he would even laugh during some of his sessions. One day he tried to tell me a joke. Slowly I began to notice that along with my stubbornness to stay with him, rain or shine, there was another person in his life who was helping him to make a better adjustment to his psychotic personality organisation. This man, let us call him Mr. Wiley, was the previous Methodist minister whom Attis replaced. He was older than Attis and had remained in the area after his retirement and after Attis took over his job. Obviously, he was much older than I. But slowly I noticed how

Attis had fused my "good" image with the image of Mr. Wiley. On a few occasions he called me Dr. Wiley instead of Dr. Volkan. One day when he came to his session he kept looking at my face in silence for a long time. Then he declared that Wiley and I looked alike. I did not interfere with his fusing me with Wiley.

In the second year as an outpatient Attis could not wait to come to his sessions in order to report how Wiley had been nice to him, how they did this or that together. I learned that the older man loved to play golf and invited Attis to join him and become a golfer. Attis' sessions were filled with his descriptions of how he would try different golf clubs, how he would hit the ball in different ways. I still did not tell him that Wiley also represented my image. My supervisor told me not to interfere with Attis' having experience in real life with a "good" object image. In reality I did not know anything about playing golf. During my developmental years and my teen years in Cyprus no one in my environment was interested in this sport; it would not have come up for discussion at all. I remember that in my mid-teens a high-school classmate of mine whose family was rich and had some social connection with the ruling British authorities took me to the British governor's place in Nicosia where there was a tennis court. My friend had permission to use this court. That day he had tennis rackets and a tennis ball for us to try playing there. Soon after I stepped onto the court, however, a Cypriot Greek guard working at the governor's place appeared, screaming at us to get off the court because we did not have proper tennis shoes. I still recall this event as a very humiliating one. Around this time, I think, I also visited my first golf course, and it may have been next to the tennis court. Tennis and golf belonged to the British elite and some very rich Greek and Turkish people, not to a Cypriot Turk like me whom the British called a "native". When Attis was talking with excitement about his golf practices and his developing love for golf, I was not emotionally with him. Sometimes I would feel bored. Obviously, I told my supervisor what Attis was talking about, but he did not seem to have curiosity about the meaning of Attis' preoccupation with golf clubs and golf balls either. He continued to inform me that Attis was having experiences with a "good" object image. To this day I do not know if my supervisor played golf himself or was interested in going to golf tournaments or watching them on television.

I wondered if the golf clubs represented Attis' detached penis, but did not share this idea with him. Only much later did I make a deeper formulation about Attis' preoccupation with golf at this time in his life. Wiley, his image also fused with mine, was helping Attis to develop a symbol and also learn about sublimation. Golf clubs stood for an axe that castrates and also for an axe that Attis could use to cut someone's throat. By learning how to play golf, Attis was not only taking the danger out of the axe, but also was learning to express his incredible childhood rage by sublimation. You do not kill anyone by playing golf; you only hit an actual ball without hurting your father's balls! I will return to this formulation later in the book.

CHAPTER EIGHT

Linking interpretations, a flesh-coloured car, and emotional flooding

As months passed, Attis' hallucinations and delusions seemed to lessen, but they did not disappear. After experiencing a confrontation with a member of his church, an especially awful "bitch", he still sensed the presence of his dead mother or father at a new cemetery, this one located closer to his new home, and Gloria's vagina again became a walrus with teeth. Perhaps he noticed my boredom with his endless golf stories. He continued to make some references to them, but now in his sessions he began a routine. He would simply tell me that he was having a bodily experience, such as neck pain. Then he would stop, give no associations, stay silent and look at me as if I knew why his neck was hurting. My inquiries as to what had triggered his bodily sensations went nowhere. Then he would tell me about a sermon he had given the previous Sunday or something about his duties at his church.

After his second year of coming to see me, Attis was coming to his sessions alone most of the time, without Gloria. One day he came to his session and described how he was in a cold sweat. He was actually sweating. Only towards the end of his session did I learn that, as he was approaching Chapel Hill, he had seen a "mean-looking" policeman in a police cruiser parked by the side of the highway. He had a thought that he might be stopped by the policeman because earlier he had been driving over the speed limit. When I heard his story about the policeman I automatically linked his cold sweat as he entered the therapy room and his noticing the "mean-looking" policeman. Soon, reporting a bodily symptom at the beginning of his session and then, during the latter part of the session referring to an event that most likely caused him to have that bodily experience became his habit. I would verbalise the connection between his reported bodily sensation and the actual event without connecting his experience with possible related genetic material such as the "mean-looking" policeman representing his sadistic father. Such exercises seemed to lead Attis towards developing better reality testing. I now know that my patient had introduced me to a technique that refers to "linking interpretations".

It was Peter Giovacchini (1969, 1972) who first described linking interpretations, and I expanded this concept further (Volkan, 1976, 1987). Giovacchini based his description of linking interpretation on Freud's (1900a) concept of *day residue* in dreams. As day residue, insignificant impressions derived from the real world—seeing a police cruiser parked at the side of a highway like Attis described, or passing a billboard depicting a smiling woman holding a milk bottle—join infantile aggressive or libidinal wishes to initiate the content of dreams. Giovacchini applied Freud's understanding of day residue to the clinical setting, stating, "An interpretation may make a casual connection by referring to the day residue which may be the stimulus for the flow of the patient's associations or for some otherwise unexplainable behaviour" (Giovacchini, 1969, p. 180). I had first noted the usefulness of linking interpretations when working with Attis, an individual with poor reality testing. Such "interpretations" link events in external reality to intrapsychic phenomena and promote contact with reality.

Here is another example of a linking interpretation I offered to another patient, Jane, who also had poor reality testing. While on my couch, she looked at the ceiling and said that blood was dripping from holes in the ceiling tiles. I connected this bizarre perception with the patient's earlier statement that she had just begun menstruating, thus linking her perception of her bleeding body with a "bleeding" environment (Volkan, 1995). At that time I did not connect her sharing about her menstruation during the session with the fact that she had been abused by her father as a child until one day he saw her menstruating and stopped abusing her. Jane was not yet ready to deal with this genetic material. Much later in her analysis she could handle her memories of abuse and work through her terrible trauma.

My playing "linking games" with Attis lasted many months until he began making such links himself, illustrating his own ability to note how external events induce bodily sensations with associated feelings and thoughts. This development was important for him in developing integrative function and psychological mindedness. I noticed how proud he was to have accomplished this. Meanwhile, some external events continued to initiate his old fears and his old ways of handling them, such as acutely and openly becoming involved in internalisation-externalisation and introjective-projective cycles. During those times, he or I, or both of us, would be "monsters", or someone else "out there" would be a "monster". Some sessions were filled with his grievances and lists of people whom he saw as agents of annihilation or castration. These experiences would make him hungry for libidinal objects to be "eaten up", and then Wiley or I would emerge as "good" object images.

After three years at Chapel Hill I finished my psychiatry residency training and moved to Goldsboro, North Carolina where I began to work as a staff psychiatrist at Cherry Hospital, which was only for African-Americans. Other physicians at Cherry Hospital were all immigrants from different countries (Volkan, 2009). Once I moved to Cherry Hospital I no longer had a supervisor in Chapel Hill. However, I continued to go to North Carolina Memorial Hospital once a week to attend some educational sessions and continued to see Attis as an outpatient. I began reading volumes of the *International Journal of Psychoanalysis* starting with Volume I; my reading replaced my sessions with a supervisor. Attis—I do not recall how—knew that I no longer lived in Chapel Hill. He seemed to express appreciation that I was still his therapist; at the same time I sensed that he perceived me as a different individual. In his sessions he appeared rather paranoid and cautious. I told him that I was the same person even though Chapel Hill was no longer my home.

Then one day when he came to see me I realised how happy he was. Before the session was over I learned that he had bought a "flesh-coloured car". I thought that this car symbolised the finger in the bottle, his detached penis, and it patched up his sense of self. This time I did not make a "linking interpretation" since he had started an event that seemed to have direct connection with his internal conflicts and since he seemed to create a symbol for his penis. I wanted to wait and see how his "flesh-coloured car" would appear in his sessions. During the following sessions I noted that the car was not yet a symbol for him; it was a protosymbol. For example, while going to a service station to have the car serviced, he would have tactile sensations on his penis whenever a serviceman raised the car's hood. Once, when the car's exhaust pipe was damaged, he actually developed haemorrhoids. I do not know how a psychological phenomenon initiates a physical bodily change but, in Attis' case, this actually occurred. Soon, he returned to a paranoid state when he felt that the car was not running well and accused the man who sold him the car of giving him an inferior vehicle.

Towards the end of the fourth year of our first meeting there was much snow in North Carolina. Attis called to cancel a number of his hours with me on the grounds that the bad weather made the trip dangerous. He offered, as an additional justification, the need to officiate at an unusual number of funerals among his parishioners. I wondered if he wanted to keep his "flesh coloured car"/penis away from me and under his control. I should not be the mother who would "steel" it and keep it in a bottle. In a general sense I imagined that the cancellations represented his wish to separate from the "early bad mother"/therapist, and the winter weather helped him to defend this wish. I concluded that he was experiencing the following fear: if he came to me, I might not only steel his car/penis, but engulf him. He seemed to fear that he might kill me, and thus himself, or part of himself which was fused with me.

When he called to cancel another session he was questioned by a new secretary about his reason for cancelling the appointment and felt great resentment over what he regarded as her aggressive curiosity. He saw her as an extension of me, the "bad mother" image, and during his next hour with me he opened the session with a complaint, albeit a calm complaint, about the secretary's pointed questions. He then began to relate a quarrel that had taken place in his hometown. The owner of a funeral home there had discontinued his ambulance service because it was unprofitable, and the townspeople were sharply critical of this curtailment of service. As he reviewed this, Attis became very angry; he spoke of what had occurred as *unjust persecution*. He felt involved in it himself inasmuch as he had been called by a community leader who suggested that the financial affairs of the mortuary needed investigation.

Attis wanted to give a sermon in support of the owner of the funeral home although this would endanger his own image in the community. In following his opening complaint about inquisitive interference over the telephone by telling of another episode involving telephone pressure, Attis did not seem to see the parallel between them: how in each a persecuting "bad" object tried to intrude on a victimised one. I did not interrupt him and continued to listen. Attis went on to say that he had recently been upset. He had returned to the habit of looking into closets for his dead father. Although he had, in the past, hallucinated his father's presence, his search now referred to a certain temper tantrum his father had had accompanied by his punitive and taunting grin. Attis was experiencing fear not only due to his "bad" mother's intentions but also his "bad" father's sadistic attitude.

Attis reported that, on his way to my office that day, he thought of turning his car around and going back home. I considered that he was afraid of losing control of his anger. He wished to protect me from his fury by thinking of not being with me. Nevertheless, he came to his appointment. But he was angered further by something that had happened as he parked his flesh-coloured car outside my office. He had located an empty spot in the crowded parking lot but had been "tricked out of it" by a "big guy" even though he had found it first. This incident triggered the anger that supported the emotions that had attended other episodes he talked about during the hour. He recalled the brother who had cut off his finger; he was angry because his brother had been his mother's favourite and she had pushed Attis into a lower place. He had been reminded at a basketball game the previous week of his boyhood prowess in athletics, which he had given up because of his mother's disapproval. There had been two brothers in the game he saw; the younger, the better player, had refrained, "for psychological reasons", from shooting the ball into the basket.

Although on the surface these incidents contained aspects of the oedipal struggle as it involved a sibling in a triangle, Attis emphasised the dyad of himself and his mother within the triangle. As Kurt Eissler (1954) long ago observed in individuals who, like Attis, have a psychotic core, an emotion can accumulate new energy by activating other memories that feed it (also see Peto, 1968).

Attis grew angrier and angrier as he poured out these memories. He was not, at this point, conscious that they were all serving to support his anger and he could not separate one event, with its accompanying feeling, from another. Suddenly he went into "emotional flooding" (Volkan, 1976, 1995), also known in the literature as "organismic panic" (Pao, 1979). Motor activity accompanied this and he moved towards me to attack. He did not hit me, and after my initial fearful surprise I found myself uttering his name. Looking back, my calling him by name was my way of giving him an identity. Apparently, not losing my therapeutic position spontaneously made me a "good object" that acknowledged him as a human being! Attis felt "paralysed" as his motor activity lapsed. I remembered how he had become catatonic when he attempted to cut Gloria's neck with an axe.

When we tried later to understand this feeling of "paralysis", he recalled the events of the night during which he had left the house in search of an axe with which to kill his wife. Although, on one level, his "paralysis" might seem a highly sophisticated defence mechanism directed by a developed superego, the patient's associations pointed to a global defence, like a primitive state of shock, a manoeuvre of "playing possum".

Patients with psychotic personality organisations resist getting well, getting rid of their psychotic core, since true wellness means visiting their internalised metaphorical doughnut filled with most unpleasant affects, experiencing and tolerating them, and then getting rid of the doughnut. Having an emotional flooding represents such a visitation. Patients do so after they have internalised the therapist's protective image and are able to keep it within themselves in a steady fashion. In other words, an emotional flooding after the patient can maintain a stable libidinal image of the therapist is a sign of major improvement.

After his emotional flooding and his paralysis were over, Attis described his emotional flooding experience as a swollen balloon saturated with unpleasant affects bursting and destroying everything within him and around him. He used the word "balloon", instead of a doughnut filled with rotten jelly! He told me that when he heard me calling his name his perception of himself as a monster gave way to a perception of himself as a groundhog. He adhered to this throughout what was left of the hour. The groundhog image is tamer than that of the monster. In layman's terms I explained to him that since he was often reminded when he was a child that he had been born on Groundhog Day, the groundhog image symbolised the core primary affective relationship between the mother and child upon which the first, but undifferentiated, self- and object images accumulated. In the following hours, he was able to feel and understand his rage against his primary love object from whom he could not obtain the needed libidinal input. This had made his separation–individuation impossible.

During his emotional flooding none of us died. I verbalised this. After this event Attis never again mentioned his wish and fear of murdering Gloria.

When I was treating Attis I was inexperienced, and also saw him only once a week. It took four years in treatment for Attis to revisit the evening he attempted to kill Gloria, and he described undergoing a "metamorphosis" during the experience. Since experiencing and tolerating an emotional flooding by a patient like Attis is the most important event in the treatment, I will briefly describe an emotional flooding by another patient. I had had more experience with individuals with psychotic personality organisation when Jane, a twenty-one-year-old college student whose case I briefly reported earlier, became my patient. I saw Jane intensively, four times a week on my couch. During her first eleven months with me Jane primarily experienced my images as "bad", and my "bad" image was involved in her internalisation–externalisation and introjective-projective cycles. Both of us tolerated this. Then I noticed her regarding me *steadily* as a new "good" object. Sitting on the couch briefly at the end of her sessions she would ask me to turn this or that way and move into or away from the light. I did not move and said nothing. She explained that she was taking my picture by blinking her eyes. I could clearly observe her becoming a camera and her blinking eyes like the shutter of a camera. When she left my presence, she went to a dark room and mentally developed my picture, externalising it onto the external world but keeping it near her. This behaviour went on for some months. Meanwhile, we were able to define my function for her as a "good" libidinal object. As a child she could not depend on her mother who was depressed due to the loss of Jane's sister, who died at the age of three when Jane was one and a half. Neither could Jane depend on her father's image. In "losing" his wife to depression he had turned to Jane and made her his target for incest.

One day on my couch Jane reported losing the boundaries of her back while lying there (representing her fusing her body image with my image). She experienced high anxiety, but not a true emotional flooding. Jane said that the couch had turned into a swimming pool and that she was floating above the water. She began moving her arms in order not to sink into the couch. She was also uncertain where her back ended and where my couch began. Sitting behind her I stayed silent and let her experience this fusing, waiting to see what would develop. The next day she lost the boundaries of her back once more while lying on the couch. But this time she had come prepared. She opened her purse and pulled out a sharp pencil and stuck it into her hand. With high anxiety she reported that she felt pain. "But", she said, "I now know that my hand and my body belong to me." She was in control of disconnecting her self-image from my image (the couch). Soon after this, Jane experienced an emotional flooding and was overwhelmed with indescribable "bad" feelings on the couch. Interestingly, this horrifying experience was accompanied by a "hallucination" of a big mouth with scary laughter coming from it. The laughter "echoed" in Jane's mind, driving her "crazy". She named her emotional flooding "Cosmic Laughter". Later we understood the nature of her specific type of emotional flooding: Her mother, who had lost Jane's sister when Jane was one and a half years old, was depressed. Even while she was pregnant with Jane she knew that her older daughter would not live because of a congenital anomaly. Furthermore, the depressed mother had a breast infection (confirmed by her mother during Jane's treatment) while nursing Jane. Because of the pain, she would abruptly remove her breast from infant Jane's mouth and then after a while, give her breast to the infant once more, and then remove it again. This interaction between the depressed mother and her baby was a faulty ingredient that was the key to the initiation of Jane's psychotic core, a doughnut filled with indescribable unpleasant affects. In the treatment, this poisonous mother/infant interaction was repeated while she was on my couch, accompanied by flooding of "bad" emotions, and was then mastered (Volkan, 1974, 1995).

In the next chapter I will describe how Attis developed a most workable transference psychosis. He became involved in a new internalisation–externalisation cycle which led to his stabilising a libidinal infantile core through stable identification with me as a new therapeutic libidinal object, replacing his psychotic core, and thus no longer possessing a doughnut or balloon full of most unpleasant affects.

CHAPTER NINE

Turkey dinners and identification with a therapeutic libidinal object

The week following his emotional flooding Attis entered my office looking very pale. He told me that the suit he was wearing was very much like one of mine; in fact, the one I wore on this occasion. In those days, since I did not have much money, I purchased my clothing off the rack. Attis could easily find the same clothing. He had had the impulse the day before to visit a clothing store and while there had purchased the suit in question, along with a shirt and tie very like my own. He also told me that he had eaten a *turkey* dinner the night before and had been anxious ever since. He knew that I had come to the United States from Turkey. Although his awareness that his imitative behaviour, his buying the new suit, had been spontaneous, he remained unaware of the meaning of his symbolic internalisation of me by eating the turkey dinner. As the hour progressed, he spoke of his fantasies of destruction directed towards me that he had entertained en route to my office. I told him that a turkey stood for my image; it was a *symbol* since I was a Turk and had come to the USA from Turkey. I added that he had a wish to resemble me by "eating me up" and his subsequent fear was that he had destroyed me by this act. I chose not to tell him that he might also want to destroy me because he was afraid that every libidinal object in his mind could turn into a destructive one. In a sense,

I "humanised" his bizarre wish to eat me. Following this exchange, he relaxed and asked what I thought about the recent Supreme Court decision about prayer in schools; he speculated about my religion. The tenor of my reply was: "Look, if you want to be like me, you need not make the resemblance an all-or-nothing business. You can get useful things from me, and you may reject other aspects of me. You can choose. You are a different person than I and, in the long run, we will continue being two different persons and continue to work together."

He wore the same lookalike clothing to our next session, saying that he had been impelled to do so. Just before we began the hour, he broke the usual routine by a trip to the bathroom where he had a hard stool. When he informed me about this he kept looking at me as if he was inquiring about something and waiting for an explanation. I explained that during the previous hour I had told him how he could choose what he wanted to keep about my image and what he wanted to get rid of. I asked him if he had a turkey dinner the night before this visit too. The answer was "yes". I told him that by defecating he tested me in order to be sure that I really meant what I had told him and added: "Once more, I tell you that it is alright to get rid of my stinking parts." He laughed.

Attis continued to eat turkey dinners and go to the bathroom just before or just after his sessions. His turkey dishes were still, to a great extent, my protosymbols (Werner & Kaplan, 1963) for him. I verbalised the difference between a protosymbol and a symbol. Upon this, Attis recalled having a fantasy some time ago after having a hard stool that he was getting rid of his father's appendix/penis from his belly. He had a similar fantasy in a bathroom after defecating just before his session with me. He told me this with a big smile on his face, and added that his father's appendix/penis was now gone forever, and he would no longer think of having it in his stomach. Around this time, Attis thought about his own death. I reminded him of his wish and attempts to "kill" unwanted things in himself, from his father's appendix, to his mother's/father's and my unwanted aspects. When he stopped completely fusing with them he would stop thinking of his own death.

I noted that Attis was developing a genuine understanding of what a symbol was; it was not identical with the thing it represented. He brought a dream to his next session. He would, as the reader knows, talk about his visual hallucinations, but this was the first time that he reported a dream. In the dream he was holding a golf club. Then he noticed that the club turned into an axe. This confused him. Then the axe became a golf club again and he felt comfortable. There was a day residue for his dream. Wiley was moving to California to a retirement place not far away from his married daughter. The day before Attis had his dream parishioners of his church had gathered there with food and drink to say goodbye to their former minister. Attis gave a speech counting the good things Wiley had done for his community and when he finished his speech he hugged the older man. Now I clearly understood how Attis, by spending time with golf clubs, was also learning how to make an axe not dangerous. He and I could now see that the golf club that Wiley had introduced to him stood as a symbol that he had tamed. When we talked about this Attis murmured, "A golf club is a golf club!" Wiley moved away and Attis continued to play golf.

After the events I described above, one day, with great pleasure, Attis told me of a sensation of getting out of his shell, developing a new personality. He wanted to take a long vacation trip and explore wider and wider areas. In my mind I visualised a groundhog that was going to explore its surroundings, sunshine or rain. Attis talked about his imagining my immigration to the United States from Turkey as a highly adventurous undertaking. Unlike me, he added, all of his life, he had been confined within a limited geographical area. He had never travelled outside the state of North Carolina in which he was born. I thought that this was not an accident but a reflection of his pathological makeup. It reflected his difficulty in separation–individuation. He could not leave his state/mother. Developing new personality, however, should now allow Attis to try to individuate away from the representation of his mother. He continued to express a desire to travel out of his state and have "adventures". He could do so through keeping the "good" aspects of turkeys he had eaten. He also said that I was not really a turkey, I was a person, and he smiled.

In one of his next sessions, Attis set Pennsylvania as his travel objective; this did, in fact, involve a considerable journey for him. His associations centred on the Liberty Bell in Philadelphia. Here I will not dwell on the history of how this bell, which weighs 2000 pounds and which was cast in London in the mid-seventeenth century, became the main icon of American independence. I felt that for Attis the Liberty Bell indicated a need for *symbolic* celebration of his "rebirth". As we discussed the proposed trip to Philadelphia, I mentioned having once made the trip there myself, implying that it was not a journey that involved any danger. In retrospect, I suspect that I sensed in him anxiety about finding his liberty and that my remark was in response to this. I needed to protect him—and, perhaps, myself within him—through such reassurance. My response was determined by my countertransference, but I think it was a proper one. At this time I did not know that Attis' brother who had amputated his finger was living not far from Philadelphia with his family. Attis had not mentioned this fact to me.

Before long, Attis did take a six-week vacation to Philadelphia and Gloria accompanied him. When he returned to see me he seemed excited. Right away he focused on the Liberty Bell and seeing the crack on it. As far as I could find out there is disagreement about when the crack first appeared on the Liberty Bell. There is a strong opinion that it originally cracked when first rung after the bell was brought to Philadelphia. In fact, the last names of two workmen who re-cast the bell appear on it. With a big smile Attis declared: "I know what a symbol is! When I noticed the crack on the bell first I thought that the bell stood for my cut finger/penis. Then, it stood for my freedom. Even though there is a crack on the bell people come to see it. It is so important."

Then there was a silence, during which I think both of us celebrated Attis owning his penis. After this Attis never had a delusion or a thought about Gloria's vagina turning into a walrus. He also stopped thinking and believing that his parents would come out of their graves and hunt him.

Attis informed me that his elder brother who had amputated his finger lived with his family near Philadelphia. The two brothers had not been in close contact for decades. On his return journey Attis and Gloria visited Attis' brother and his family. "I wanted to show him my 'new personality'," Attis said. I realised that his choosing to visit Philadelphia was what Samuel Novey (1968) called a "second look". Novey described how after working through some internal problems, some patients go to their childhood locations and/or talk with adults who were around during their childhood to collect information to verify their newly gained insights and internal changes. Attis did not go to his childhood location, but to Philadelphia where there is a bell with a crack in it, and where the brother who had amputated one of his fingers lived nearby. Philadelphia was a place where he would have a "second look" experience.

Before telling the story of Attis after his trip to Philadelphia, let us return to his eating turkey dinners and visits to bathrooms. From the time I had met him there had been many examples of his internalisation–externalisation cycles. In Chapter Five I wrote about how individuals with psychotic personality organisation defend themselves from experiencing overwhelming anxiety or emotional flooding by externalisation-internalisation and also by further fragmentation, further fusion-diffusion, further projection-introjection, and/ or wiping out more reality. But it is also true that, after "testing" the therapist's image long enough, the patient utilises the internalisation-externalisation cycles as the point where he catches a chance to begin to change his internal world and get rid of his psychotic core. After experiencing and tolerating an emotional flooding, Attis could more easily choose and keep libidinal object images within and *identify* with them, and externalise only aggressively tinged object images. His eating of turkey dinners and getting rid of my unwanted aspects through his rectum stabilised selected libidinal aspect of my image in him. This furthered the turning point in his treatment.

In the next chapter I will examine internalisation–externalisation and accompanying introjection-projection cycles in a treatment process, by giving examples from two other cases in order to further illustrate various functions of such cycles, including a patient's collecting libidinal images within and identifying with them, thus modifying his psychotic core and saying goodbye to the psychotic personality organisation.

CHAPTER TEN

Internalisation–externalisation cycles and the alteration of the psychotic core

In 'Three essays on the theory of sexuality' Sigmund Freud (1905d) referred to the experience of sucking as an essential gratification tied to the oral zone and linked with nutrition. Although Freud (1887–1902) mentioned "identification" in his letters to Wilhelm Fliess, it was in *Three Essays* that he wrote about the sexual aim of the oral phase (oral incorporation of the object) which became a prototype of identification. Adapting the terms "introject" and "introjections" from Sándor Ferenczi (1909), Freud applied them to the analysis of mourning and melancholia (Freud, 1917e), which signalled the beginnings of the concept of internalised object images. Mourning refers to an obligatory preoccupation with the internalised images of a dead person or lost thing. The Kleinian school should receive the credit for carrying the study of object relatedness and the internalisation of objects—at the outset, part of objects—back to the beginnings of life experiences. As Otto Kernberg's (1969) review of the Kleinian formulations also shows, this school influenced what was then the mainstream of psychoanalysis to focus further on the earliest level of relatedness. Internalisation–externalisation of self- and object images (accompanied by introjection and projections of affects and thoughts as the infant and child grow up), the earliest type of relatedness for everyone, inevitably reappears prominently in the process of treating persons like Attis. This was noticed long ago by many analysts (for example see: Searles, 1951; Hoedemaker, 1955; Limentani, 1956; Szasz, 1957; Abse & Ewing, 1960; Cameron, 1961; Boyer, 1967).

For some time the experiences a patient like Attis has with external objects may provide him with little new material, since the appearance of his primitive relatedness causes him to perceive whatever he internalises as representatives of archaic objects. Initially, the therapist's image does not provide the patient with an analytical attitude that he may use as a characterological modality of his own. It is up to the therapist to differentiate herself at the outset from the archaic object images, in piecemeal fashion, in order to help her patient alter his internal world.

Since the reactivation of primitive relatedness to objects naturally leads the patient to internalise his therapist, any manoeuvre of the therapist to offer himself openly to his patient with a psychotic core as a model is usually a seductive intrusion that may lead to extreme anxiety. Some early analysts, noticing the patient's internalisation–externalisation cycles and their libidinal object hunger, seemed to have had a wish to offer themselves to their patients as "good" objects and were involved in actions that were desperate efforts to respond to patients' needs. For example, I recall reading how Marguerite Sechehaye (1951) put two green apples on her breasts and offered the apples as a symbol of herself to her patient, Renée. We should remember Harold Searles (1951) stating that the "incorporative processes" within the transference–countertransference relationship with an individual with psychotic personality organisation, when used as a defence against overwhelming anxiety, can be the basis of many stalemates in psychoanalytic therapy.

During their analytic treatment we notice that individuals with higher level personality organisations also use the internalisation–externalisation process, but usually such cycles are hidden behind more complex interactions between the patient and the analyst, unless the patient regresses a great deal, whether it is in the service of progression or not. Sometimes internalisation–externalisation relatedness appears in neurotic patients' dreams. In fact, internalisation–externalisation cycles are at the foundation of each psychoanalytic process. Therefore, when we think of a description of any psychoanalytic process we need to make a reference to internalisation–externalisation cycles and their resulting in new healthy identifications.

James Strachey was one of the first psychoanalysts who, in 1934, offered a metapsychology of psychoanalytic technique. Of course, at that time he was not dividing the analysands' personality organisations into different categories, as I have illustrated in this book. Later, Strachey's ideas were modified and expanded by many analysts who came after him. Briefly, the focus of Strachey's metapsychology is internalisation-externalisation and accompanying introjection-projection processes that take place during analytic work. The analyst does not return the analysand's externalisations and projections right away, and thus through her analytic stance modifies them before giving them back to the patient. The analyst becomes, according to Strachey, an *auxiliary superego*. Such a process, through identifications, changes the patient's severe superego.

Following Strachey, in 1956 Paula Heimann described how the analyst becomes an *auxiliary ego*. Heimann tells us to imagine an infant who first shrinks from a new object, a cat, and takes flight into his mother's arms. After the mother gently strokes the cat's back and shows the infant that the creature is not dangerous, the infant, encouraged by his mother, does the same thing. The old terms "auxiliary superego" and "auxiliary ego" refer to the analyst as a *new object, analytic introject*, or *developmental object*—terms used by analysts of later years (Szasz, 1957; Loewald, 1960; Cameron, 1961; Giovacchini, 1972; Kernberg, 1975; Volkan, 1976; Tähkä, 1993; Volkan & Ast, 1994). The analyst's newness does not refer to his or her social existence in the real world, but depends on the analyst being an object (and its representation) not hitherto encountered. The patient's interaction with a "new object" is akin to a nurturing child–mother relationship (Rapaport, 1951; Ekstein, 1966).

Attis' internalisation–externalisation cycles became "therapeutic" when he started to eat turkey prior to his visits with me and when he felt uncomfortable "defecating" selected aspects of my image. In this chapter I will give examples of internalisation–externalisation processes, accompanied by introjections and projections of affects and thoughts of two other patients with psychotic personality organisation. I do this in order to provide the reader with a better understanding and appreciation of Attis' way of being stuck in such relatedness for a long time before utilising the same relatedness to change his internal world. The following cases are from a time in my life when I had become a more experienced therapist and when I could see my patients more intensively during their treatments.

Sharon, in her late twenties, was a beautiful woman who had a psychotic core. She was the daughter of an extremely narcissistic woman and an ineffectual man who had inherited a huge amount of money. The family had no financial concerns and lived in an enormous home. Sharon had two older sisters and was born eight years after her second sister. Her mother was very upset when she realised that she was once more pregnant. Before Sharon was born—as Sharon heard her mother tell it again and again while she was growing up—her mother often sat naked in the family room in front of a huge mirror and adored her body. Her husband, her two children and one of the family maids were allowed to be in the room with her when she was naked. She told them that she did not wish her belly be swollen again by pregnancy. She thought of abortion, but she did not go through with it. Sharon was definitely an unwanted child. After she was born, her mother again began to sit naked in front of the mirror. This time she noticed that her pregnancy with Sharon had caused some wrinkles to appear on her abdomen. She hated Sharon because of this. She gave up sitting naked during the daytime a few months after Sharon was born.

It appears that the family members dealt with her hated existence in a most bizarre fashion by attempting to make Sharon pure and thus acceptable. From Sharon's very early childhood onwards, her mother, her father, and even her two older sisters gave Sharon enemas almost daily. If Sharon exhibited confusion or anxiety she would receive enemas more than once a day. This went on and on. By the time I met Sharon I had heard enough bizarre stories about childrearing that learning the facts of Sharon's upbringing did not shock me. Often, individuals with severe mental problems come to see clinicians under the impression that only biology, genetics, or neurological issues cause patients' conditions. This is a big mistake.

When she was age fifteen Sharon wrapped a piece of faecal material in a tissue and presented it to a sister in the family room where the other members of the family were present. After this episode the enemas were discontinued. On the surface Sharon appeared "normal". After high school she attended a college, but left it without graduating. When I listened to her description of her high school and college days, in my mind, I perceived her as a "beautiful doll" with limited emotional expressions and logical mind. At the age of twenty-five, she married a man who was the son of another rich man and who, with the help of one of his father's able assistants, had an administrative job in his father's business. I guessed that he wanted to possess a "beautiful doll" and so he married Sharon.

Soon after her marriage Sharon's primitive object relationship became very obvious. She persuaded her husband to give her an enema before sex and she became addicted to sleeping pills. Her analytic treatment started a few years after her marriage when her addiction to enemas and pills increased and when she supposedly exhibited some catatonic spells, such as staying "frozen" in front of a mirror. I imagined that she was imitating her mother for some psychological purpose. She did not tell me about this symptom. I started to work with her four times a week. In spite of her physical beauty she appeared to me at times to be little more than a gastrointestinal tube as she lay on my couch. She would try to arouse in me a desire to intrude within her body; at the same time she feared such intrusion. She perceived her analysis as an enema experience, feeling that the analyst would go to work in her entrails. She therefore needed to protect herself from internalising my image as a "bad", intrusive object. Her experiences with enemas were condensed with her primal scene fantasies and on the couch she illustrated a kind of "reaching up" (Boyer, 1961, 1983; Volkan, 1976, 1997, 2010), talking endlessly of sexualised desires and dreads.

In the eighth month of Sharon's treatment I took a two-week holiday, during which I more clearly became the non-caring mother. When our work resumed she would simply lie on the couch and speak almost exclusively about her typical daily activities: staying home, placing an enema tube in her rectum, watching television, and sometimes masturbating. I sensed that placing an enema tube in her rectum was reassurance that she was in control of whatever went into or came out of her body/soul. One day, just before she ended her session, Sharon urinated on my couch, but only a little. During those days I had a couch covered with plastic. I did not know what to say or what to do for a few minutes. Then I asked her to go to the bathroom near my office, get some wet and dry paper towels, come back to my office, wipe off the urine and then dry the plastic. Without hesitation she did this. The next day she urinated on my couch again. This time she had come well-prepared; she had brought her cleaning supplies. I told her that our work's magic was to put her wishes and dreads, and especially her bodily impulses in words during our sessions. I explained that I could maintain my curiosity better when I heard words describing her impulse to urinate on my couch, than wondering about who would clean my couch. She did not urinate on my couch again.

Soon, I noticed that she would secretly chew on something while on my couch. When whatever she had in her mouth was chewed away she would put a new thing in her mouth while trying to hide her action from me. After some days I expressed my curiosity of her new actions on the couch. I learned that what she was popping into her mouth were ring-shaped mints that were sold as *Life Savers*. I sensed that her Life Savers were protosymbols: as long as she had one in her mouth, my "bad" image could not enter her; her life would be saved. Sharon's use of Life Savers continued for a few months, until one day she declared that she no longer needed them. She now had sweet candies in her mouth. I understood that her fear of internalising my image was no longer a matter of psychological life and death for her, and that now I was somewhat different from her archaic destructive object images, which were most likely linked to her aggressive self-fragments externalised onto me. I explained her internalisation and did not refer to her externalisation; in other words, I focused on what was terrifying her—the notion that my "coming in" might destroy her viscera. I wanted to wait before mentioning how she also had aggressive feelings that she put into me. Her chewing candies continued for some months despite my explanations. When I sensed that her attitude was more relaxed, I suggested that we might try to work without anything in her mouth. If she did not like something I said or did she could feel free to speak about it. She was somewhat flooded with emotions during the next session, but not disorganised. She told me that she did not have anything in her mouth. We began a new phase, so to speak, of her treatment.

Soon, however, Sharon's father-in-law assigned her husband to an administrative job in London. He also assigned his able assistant to guide his son's work there. I was informed that the family had found a new therapist for Sharon in England. I lost my patient. Four years later I received a very brief note from Sharon's husband, with no return address. It simply stated that Sharon's therapy with her new therapists, several of them, had not been successful and that she had committed suicide. I still recall my shock, sadness, and feelings of helplessness with an accompanying idea that if I had continued working with her she would still be alive, even hopefully with self-esteem and without a psychotic core.

While Sharon's case illustrates internalisation–externalisation in a most obvious way, I did not have a chance to see if she would "move up" and identify with me as a "new object". Ricky, the next patient I will describe, also began his treatment with me by illustrating his internalisation–externalisation cycle with bodily actions. In working with him over the years I would very clearly see the changing functions of his cycle and his move to a level in which his aggression-filled psychotic core was replaced by a libidinal one. Another reason why I chose to write about Ricky is the fact that he had a deformity with his fingers. Thus, I connect his case with that of Attis. In some ways, as the reader will see, Ricky and Attis, as children, shared certain psychological positions, such as the illusion that their mother had the power to correct their physical deformities but never would.

Ricky was an eighteen-year-old when I first saw him. I worked with him in my office at the University of Virginia Hospital in Charlottesville, Virginia where I had seen Sharon. After staying in North Carolina for five years I had moved to Virginia and become a faculty member of the Department of Psychiatry at the University of Virginia School of Medicine. I received the following information from Ricky's referring psychiatrist: Ricky was born with a deformed right hand and foot, his right fingers and toes being much shorter than the left ones. Beginning on his fourth birthday, his mother started giving him "wedding rings" for birthday presents. These rings were large and would not fit his deformed fingers. The mother never talked openly with Ricky about his congenital deformity. The referring psychiatrist was aware that the mother was incapable of teaching Ricky what was real and what was unreal. When Ricky was in high school a girl casually told him that his voice sounded different. He interpreted this to mean that girls might think that another part of his body, his penis, might be deformed too. Soon after this incident he developed overt psychotic symptoms. He read every book he could find about Nazi Germany. His ideal did not appear to be Adolf Hitler himself, but Hitler's "right arm", Joseph Goebbels, who in reality had a deformed leg. Thinking of his mother as Hitler and himself as Goebbels, Ricky thought that he could intimidate everybody. The referring psychiatrist told me that this was the way Ricky was attempting to deal with his castration anxiety. He added that Ricky was submissive to his tyrannical mother, as Goebbels had been submissive to Hitler. When Ricky reached the age of sixteen, his mother gave him the usual gift of a golden wedding ring for his birthday. The next day his parents committed him to a state hospital. The referring psychiatrist worked at this state hospital and looked after Ricky who was placed in a ward with other mentally troubled youngsters. The psychiatrist told me that Ricky was given medication. Whenever he had time the psychiatrist would talk with Ricky and tell him that in reality he was not castrated. At the hospital, Ricky's psychological condition improved. He no longer talked about Hitler and Goebbels. His psychiatrist, however, noticed that Ricky kept walking with an erect stance like a Nazi soldier would have done. The psychiatrist thought that holding his body in an erect position while walking was Ricky's way of denying his castration—he was making his body an erect penis. Ricky was discharged and I was asked to treat him as an outpatient.

Listening to the physician, I realised that I was hearing another bizarre story of how a mother had related to her child, most likely in order to deny her narcissistic hurt, anger, and guilt for giving birth to a child with a physical deformity. I sensed that Ricky had more problems than anxiousness about feeling castrated. I thought that his obsession with the Nazis, calling his mother Hitler and himself Goebbels, might be linked to a doughnut with "bad" jelly sitting in the middle of his soul.

During my first two sessions I noted how Ricky held his body erect and rigid. Yes, the referring physician was right. He was walking like the Nazi soldiers parading in front of Hitler! He was interested in inanimate objects in my office, such as paintings on my office walls and my books on the bookshelf. I sensed that he was trying to familiarise himself in these new surroundings. During the middle of his third hour with me Ricky suddenly stopped talking, his eyelids appeared heavy and he started to make sucking movements with his lips. After a while I thought that he was also making spitting motions and sounds. I said to myself: "You are observing the most concrete and drastic internalisation-externalisation event of your career."

A sign with my name on it was attached to the side of my door opening to a corridor outside. There were three more offices of other physicians also with doors opening to the same corridor, also with name signs. Ricky told me that he had read my name, Vamık Volkan, again before coming in for his third session. He concluded that I was a German and "as strong as Hitler". Obviously he had noticed my accent and sensed that I was not originally from America. He informed me that he was drinking and spitting out German wine. If he were a patient with a neurotic personality organisation I would most likely have said nothing and waited to hear more of his remarks about me. It was important to create a "reality base" for Ricky, so I said: "I am not German; I am an ethnic Turk." Without any hesitation he asked me: "Do Turks make wine too?" I responded: "Yes." He then asked his second question: "Do Turks make sweet wine or sour wine?" I said: "Both," and added, "You have a choice. You can choose whichever you want." Ricky chose the sweet Turkish wine and with a more obvious mouth motion and deep sound he took in a big sip of it and seemed relaxed. I was thankful to Attis for being my first teacher and introducing me to the fact that some patients in obligatory fashion, openly and in bizarre ways present eating and spitting out object and/or self-images.

I will not give details of Ricky's case or his treatment. My only purpose is to tell stories to illustrate changing functions and aims of his internalisation–externalisation cycles associated with changing introjections and projections of affects and thoughts during his treatment with me.

Sometime after drinking sweet Turkish wine during his third session Ricky heard an internal voice with a Turkish accent, which would tell him what to do. But he also had another internal voice with a German accent telling him not to listen to the first voice. Hearing these two internal voices continued for many, many months. When my internalised object image competed with his "Hitler mother" image Ricky would often became flustered. I told him that there was no rush to choose between the two voices and that the voice with the Turkish accent was rather new to him. I added that surely he was not yet sure if this Turkish voice would be helpful to him. He should take his time to test and get to know this new voice.

During the second year of his treatment I learned that Ricky had replaced his preoccupation with books on Nazi Germany with an interest in history books about Turks. However, his learning that Turks had a reputation as "terrible warmongers" confused him. He could not differentiate a "terrible Turk" from a Nazi German. This situation, I sensed, put a buffer between us. During his sessions he would whistle so that my image and voice would not be heard and would not be internalised or introjected through his ears. He was like Sharon with her Life Saver or candy in her mouth. I tolerated his whistling sessions long enough before I asked him to stop whistling so that both of us could experience what would happen and try to put our understanding of it into words.

I added that he was free to tell me when he perceived me as a scary person and that I had no intention of killing him as I had no power to make his fingers and toes longer.

After his whistling stopped I noticed that he was using my image as a libidinalising object. He began imagining eating "Turkish delights". As his "Turkish delight" he began using me as someone who would teach him reality testing. Did I know the exact distance between Charlottesville and Washington? At first I replied directly and told him the exact distance. Then I asked him to find out the answers so that he could develop his autonomy. When he resisted this, I dealt with the resistance by telling him, for example, that if he figured out the distance between Charlottesville and Washington by himself and reported it to me I would still be around and not leave him. In fact, we could then experience a relationship between two knowledgeable individuals, which, I explained, might be exciting and pleasurable.

At times Ricky would sexualise his "eating" of a Turkish delight and behave as if he was submitting to me sexually. Slowly this behaviour reflected his development of a "neurotic" father transference. He moved up to identify with more mature and sophisticated analyst functions, and gave up his psychotic symptoms and preoccupation with the Nazis. Meanwhile, he finished his high school studies and became a university student. Some months later he started dating a young woman and his analysis came to an end.

CHAPTER ELEVEN

Workable transference

After returning from Philadelphia, Attis behaved as if he were born again. But an external event would make him anxious that his newborn "self" would be treated like the original one who had been under the shadow of his early mother. In the waiting room before one of his sessions, he overheard several office personnel speaking about my having a new baby girl. I was married during my first year of psychiatric residency in Chapel Hill and what Attis overheard was true. I had never mentioned to him that I was married and he had not known of my wife's pregnancy. Without meaning to do so, the office personnel had provided him with a readymade suitable event to trigger memories of his earlier life history. Instead of becoming fragmented and involved in exaggerated defensive internalisation–externalisation cycles, Attis' examination of his early life experiences this time looked like an examination of similar issues by a person with higher-level personality organisation.

In the session after Attis found out about my new baby, he repeatedly referred to my newborn, calling her "him", although he was aware that the child was female. Attis also reminded me of how amused he had been during his visit to his older brother, only four years his senior, when his brother had several times called him "son". I sensed that he was behaving as if he were my newborn child; he was being "born" again. In the following sessions I noticed that the psychological impact of his hearing that I had a new baby had changed. This time my baby represented for Attis his younger siblings, the twins, a boy and a girl, and his youngest sister with hearing difficulty. As he did in his childhood, he now had to compete with a sibling(s) born after him and face a mother/therapist who would not have time to take care of him and love him.

While I did not deny that, indeed, I had a newborn baby in my home, I told Attis that it might be unfortunate that the office personnel had allowed him to hear something about my life. Back then, without today's incredible communication technology, psychoanalytic therapists could easily manage to keep facts of their private lives away from their patients. Today when patients become preoccupied with a therapist's private life they may learn about it through the internet or Facebook, using such information as a focus for resistance against examining their own internal worlds. When this happens, the therapist needs to say something like this to the patient: "I know that you are very curious about me. This is expected. We meet in this room four times a week. Allow yourself to get to know me as we interact in this room. Your inquiring about my life outside of this room will interfere with our relationship in the service of understanding your wishes, dreads, and conflicts, your internal world; it may make our psychological travelling together in this room difficult." Such remarks, without accusing or humiliating the patient, help them to develop a more workable transference relationship.

Now, returning to Attis, I suggested that, due to what we knew of his childhood, the knowledge of my baby might be burdensome to him. Then I added that we could turn this development between us into an opportunity for examining together his early disappointments in life and render their impact on him harmless. Being aware that he had transferred his disappointment and rage with his early mother onto me, I wanted him to know that I was in full control of my faculties and prepared to continue with his treatment. He felt somewhat relaxed but, in spite of this, after this session he went to an internist for a thorough medical check-up. I felt that he sought the examination for psychological reasons, wanting reassurance that his "new personality" was indeed a healthy one and that his murderous rage about my having a daughter would not return to him and damage him.

My becoming his early mother in the transference continued. Was he playing second fiddle to my new baby? Would I be able to give him my attention now that I had a new baby at home to distract me? He was also exhibiting an "observing ego", even though it was not yet firmly established. Both of us recalled again and again how he had had to play "second fiddle" in competition for his mother's attention when the twins and his deaf sister were born. Sometime later he returned to the feeling that he was a newborn child—an adult with a new personality. His transference manifestations reflected his anxiety that the newborn "son" might face castration by his mother or her agent as the original son.

I was surprised to hear that Attis had recently become president of his district ministerial association. I realised that as he, without the impact of a psychotic core, was able to work on the psychological problems between us, he had become freer from his disturbing symptoms while performing his duties at his church. His transference expectation that the mother/therapist might castrate him resulted in his idea of giving up his new position of honour—a self-castration proposed to control the castration he felt I might inflict on him. He ceased having sexual relations with Gloria. His old flesh-coloured car once more became "alive", a penis. He wanted to sell it in another gesture of self-castration. When he began playing golf with Mr. Wiley he would, at times, be petrified to put his fingers in a hole to retrieve a ball, thinking that a small creature in the hole might eat them. Wiley's kindness had helped him to get rid of this symptom, but now it returned. Putting his fingers in a hole would induce in him severe anxiety and he would then develop psychosomatic disturbances such as diarrhoea or stomach aches. In fact, he periodically abandoned golf, and it would take some months before he found the courage to play again. However, at the same time that Attis was having these thoughts and experiences concerning self-castration or castration by others, he was also maintaining his "observing ego" to some extent, and was aware of the reasons for his thoughts and activities. What a change! He was aware that he had two visions about me: I was a new, non-threatening object, standing by him and exploring his internal world with him, and I was also a representative of his scary early mother. He brought two dreams to his two consequent sessions. In the first one his old friend Wiley appeared. Wiley held Attis' arm in a friendly way and they walked onto a golf course. Once on the golf course Attis found himself half-naked with a big erect penis between his legs. There were happy rabbits freely jumping around. Attis also started to jump up and down happily. He turned around and saw me, instead of Wiley, with an approving smile on my face. A week later in his dream I turned into a "bitch".

According to Wilfred Abse and John Ewing (1960), "The inevitable introjection of the therapist [by a person with psychotic personality organisation] is itself partly corrective insofar as this introject competes with the archaic introject of the tyrannical mother" (p. 508). Harold Searles (1986) expressed a similar view when he spoke of experiences of jealousy involving an internal object. Attis' old unloving and tyrannical mother image actively competed with my new analytic object image. Sometimes Attis speculated as to which would be victorious. He could not integrate his two visions of me; my self-representation was split into a "good" one and a "bad" one, but not fragmented into many pieces. In those days there was no in-depth investigation of the diagnostic category known today as a "borderline" condition. Especially after Otto Kernberg's work (1975, 1988) psychoanalysts and psychodynamic therapists began studying borderline patients and their split internal worlds.

Attis decided that his mother had been like Soviet leader Nikita Khrushchev, regarded at that time in America as an aggressively invested "bad" object representation, and the brother who had "castrated" him resembled Fidel Castro. Attis' talk about Khrushchev and Castro, I thought, reflected his interest in finding a more widened external world, and his increased ability to find and maintain symbols. His therapist was from Turkey, which was on the side of the United States. I sensed that he had been reading news about Turkey. I did not ask him a question about this because I did not wish to interfere with his developing ego function related to expanding his knowledge about the external world. He reported that, although his mother had warned him not to trust strangers (foreigners), he felt that he could trust me.

In a later session, when I was a "good" object for him, Attis was able to express gratitude to me for saving him from "fire", his metaphorical doughnut filled with aggression. He recalled that, when his mother had saved him from the burning house and, later, when she had "preserved" his penis (the finger in the bottle), obligation to her had necessitated his being in her shadow, unindividuated, and remaining ill.

For some months Attis alternated between trusting me and thinking that I might still be like his archaic object images. He wondered if I would demand total submission of his new self to me. His mother had stolen his penis, although at the same time she had preserved it. He was afraid of freedom from her lest she destroy it. In a new transference situation, he saw me as a homosexual and began to refer to me as such during several sessions. Rather than focusing on his externalisation and projection of aspects of his old hermaphrodite image onto me, I interpreted the early mother transference. If I were a homosexual, I would emulate his mother in keeping his penis. Once more, I helped him to differentiate between his mother representation and the new analytic object. I also explained to him why he was having difficulty in integrating my mental images and then perceiving me as someone who is basically the same person all the time. I referred to his anxiety that if he put together "good" and "bad" therapist, the latter one may destroy the first one. I told him that I was the same person all the time. However, I was not in hurry for him to see me in the same way. This would happen slowly. I asked him to continue to observe this process with me.

I was hopeful that when the new analytic object was rendered less dangerous by my explanations and interpretations, Attis could identify with its enriching functions selectively. Slowly but steadily, within a year he began to maintain his new and rather integrated sense of self most of the time; I sensed that he relinquished his psychotic core more effectively. But, still, he kept split images of me. Our work was by no means complete. Then I moved away, to a new state, to Virginia.

In early 1963, when I had completed my two-year obligation to work at state hospitals in North Carolina, I came to Charlottesville as a new faculty member at the University of Virginia. I was in the Department of Neuropsychiatry, since at that time the departments of psychiatry and neurology were combined. One of my supervisors at Chapel Hill was Wilfred Abse who had been accepted as a professor of psychiatry in Charlottesville, and with his help I also obtained a position there.

Just before I told Attis about my upcoming relocation he was attempting to relate to me as a strong father figure who could help him, through the mechanism of identification with the aggressor (A. Freud, 1936) to intrapsychically separate further from his early mother's representation. I discussed my new position at the University of Virginia with him, explaining that my own realities had convinced me to move to another state. I explained where we were in his treatment and gave him the name of a therapist I knew from my psychiatric residency days who then had an office in a town not far from where Attis and Gloria lived. I moved to Charlottesville with an increased self-esteem due to the fact that my years-long dream of being a teacher had finally come true.

The chairperson of the psychiatry department in Charlottesville would not become a figure for identification for me as a scholar. He was a nice man whose main interest was reincarnation. He travelled around the globe interviewing people whom he considered to be reincarnated individuals. A few years after I became a faculty member at the University of Virginia I was invited to a psychiatric meeting in Adana, Turkey. While in Adana, I learned that my chairperson had already been in this Turkish city on several occasions. Local people had chosen a boy and "educated" him to be a reincarnated figure of a man who had died some time before. As "proof" of the boy's reincarnation, they focused on a birthmark on his face that was apparently similar to one the dead man also had. I learned that the department chairperson had an "agent" in Istanbul searching for reincarnated individuals in Turkey. The people in Adana, through this agent, had invited the chairperson to come to Adana and, for a fee that represented a huge sum for local people, to study the "reincarnated" boy. After I learned this story I further distanced myself from the chairperson. Soon he left his position but remained a faculty member in the department. With a huge grant and with the help of a few assistants, he would continue to investigate reincarnation. The new chairperson, who also came to Charlottesville from University of North Carolina, was a psychoanalyst. I received United States citizenship on 4 July 1968 at Monticello, Thomas Jefferson's home in Charlottesville. Soon I also received a modest grant and began my psychoanalytic training at the Washington Psychoanalytic Institute.

A few months after I had settled in Charlottesville I received a telephone call from Attis. He told me that he had decided not to continue with the psychiatrist to whom I had referred him. Working with this therapist, he added, was not at all like working with me. He used a psychiatric term—I do not know how he learned it—to tell me that he had "regressed". He informed me that he wanted to drive to Charlottesville to meet with me once a month. Doing this, he was sure, would be better than my referring him to yet another therapist, and he wanted me to understand his determination. He would not seek treatment from anyone else, and was sure that coming to see me would prevent his "regression", I accepted and we began to meet in

Charlottesville. We did this for decades, with less and less frequency as time passed. However, under certain conditions, such as when he was diagnosed with heart problems in his seventies, I was always willing to see him more frequently. Attis would never return to a psychotic disorganisation. Indeed, his visits with me and sometimes his telephone calls to me prevented his regression. During the first dozen years after my move to Charlottesville he made an adaptation to life at a borderline personality level; he became my "satellite".

CHAPTER TWELVE

Satellite state and therapeutic play

According to Greek mythology, master craftsman Daedalus, imprisoned on Crete, found that escape from the island would be difficult since King Minos was keeping watch by sea and offering a large reward for his capture. To escape, Daedalus crafted a pair of wings for himself and another for his son Icarus, made from feathers held in place with wax. At the moment of escape, Daedalus warned his son not to soar too high, lest the sun melt the wax, nor swoop too low, lest the feathers be wetted by the sea (Graves, 1957). Icarus disobeyed his father's instructions and began soaring towards the sun. The heat melted the wax holding the wings together, and Icarus fell into the sea and drowned.

The dangers of flying higher than the father, indicating problems at the oedipal level, have received much attention in psychoanalytic literature. For example, Douglas Danford Bond's (1952) study of military pilots during World War II indicated that Icarian fantasies were extremely common among fliers who developed phobias about flying. According to this author, many pilots who had flying phobias regarded the renunciation of flying as equivalent to a self-executed castration.

In referring to Attis' case, let us focus on Daedalus' advice that Icarus should not swoop too low lest the feathers be wetted and he would plunge into the sea. Icarian fantasies of this latter type mainly refer to unresolved separation–individuation problems. During the first years after I moved to Charlottesville, Attis came to see me once a month and later once every two or three months. He would also telephone me on some occasions. During the second and third years after our long-distance relationship had begun, he reported dreams in which he, or a representative of himself, moved around a central object. A characteristic of these dreams was the dependent state of the satellite, which never seemed to leave its orbit. The following is an example of Attis' dreams:

> I dreamed of a huge steel ball, like the earth, and an eagle. Every
> hundred years, the eagle would fly by and brush the ball with its
> wing tip.

Earlier in this book I referred to Theodore Dorpat's (1976) statement, which describes how a desire to be close to an object and desire to be distant cannot be understood without applying a theory of object relations. Attis' associations to the above dream were associated with his relations with me and my mental representation. He told me that he was the eagle and he was doomed to spend an eternity circling around a steel ball until the steel ball was worn out, when he would be free from me who represented a combination of his early mother and a new object. Two representations were sometimes integrated and at other times unintegrated. He experienced seeing me, every month or less, on one level as if a century went by after each visit. But still he would not accept another therapist with an office closer to him. Meanwhile, usually every three years or so, the Methodist Church continued assigning him to new locations in North Carolina, even though he was no longer exhibiting bizarre behaviour. In fact, he told me that the church then thought of him as a good model for a Methodist minister.

Attis taught me how a person with a borderline personality organisation can make an "adaptation" to life by creating a "satellite state" and by controlling the maintenance of this state. Obviously, after I moved to Charlottesville, I was no longer involved in conducting a typical therapeutic process with Attis. As he had hoped, however, this new type of relationship between us, his being my satellite, was preventing the possibility of his experiencing major regression and going back to a psychotic personality organisation. As long as Attis circled around me—as he did around the church, by never totally committing himself to it and by often desiring to resign from his religious post—he functioned without clinical psychosis. He was careful to stay in an orbit around me as he was careful in his dealings with the church authorities. If he came close to me, he could be engulfed; if he went too far from me, he could be without regulatory powers. Unlike the times when I first met him, Attis was not making references to God, Jesus, or the Bible during his sessions. Once, as the reader will recall, he had tried to identify with Jesus when he had his first dramatic psychotic episode, and went through a forest to a mountaintop, surrendered to God and almost died. Now, he was not a deeply religious person. He was obviously using religious statements while performing his duty as a Methodist minister, but he sometimes informed me that he found his job at the church rather boring. He wished he had training for another kind of profession. Intrapsychically speaking, during this time in his life the church had evolved as another steel ball, primarily representing a mother figure, and he was circling round it just as he was circling around me.

It was my observation of Attis' behaviour patterns, as well as those of two other patients, that led me and Robert Corney to formulate a peculiar adjustment to life that we referred to as being in a "satellite state" (Volkan & Corney, 1968). We maintained that, in this circumstance, the clinical picture was that of a borderline case. Our formulation on the satellite state was based on Margaret Mahler's and her associates' (Mahler & Furer, 1963, 1966) description of autistic, symbiotic, and separation–individuation schema. After our paper was published, Margaret Mahler, in a letter to me, supported our formulation. We now know that an infant's mind is more active than we had thought and that "normal autism" as described by Mahler cannot be accepted. It has been reported that Mahler herself, prior to her death, had questioned some of her perceptions about the autistic period. However, her description of the symbiotic phase and the one that follows it, the separation–individuation phase, has stood up well to closer scrutiny. After the symbiotic period, the infant begins a series of overlapping advancements which, if successfully traversed, will permit him to evolve as a separate and distinct individual. These crucial times have been called the phase of separation–individuation and, in the normal child, extend, for all practical purposes, until about thirty-six months of age.

Margaret Mahler and Manuel Furer (1963, 1966) specifically state that they do not mean physical separation from mother in behavioural terms, but an intrapsychic separation which, in a normal situation, takes place in the physical presence of mother. I adhere to this definition but feel that in certain adults physical separation experiences can tip the balance, throwing into bold relief vulnerable individuals' earlier unresolved separation–individuation problems and causing clinical difficulty. In these individuals, the physical separation experience becomes primitively symbolised and represents the psychic separation experience. Such was the case when Attis experienced our physical separation between his infrequent sessions as representing a psychic separation. His ego development that existed until then now had a major task of maintaining a satellite relationship with me. I represented a new object as well as his early mother, a source of instant gratification on one hand and a source of instant pull to fusion on the other hand, and he felt obliged to orbit around me. When the centre is perceived as "good", the patient feels closeness to it, but does not come too close, fearing that the centre may turn out to be "bad". When the centre is perceived as "bad", the patient remains distant from it, but not too far distant, in case the centre may turn out to be "good" again. The need–fear dilemma (Abse & Ewing, 1960; Burnham, 1969) is handled well by the formation of a satellite position.

Corney and I came to understand satellite dreams, like those Attis had, as fulfilling two wishes. First, they permit the expression of an extreme degree of dependency without the consequent loss of identity through fusion, which would accompany their conscious recognition of this desire. Second, they keep aggression under control by permitting wishes for freedom to be expressed without interruption of the satellite state. Aggression against the representation of the mother, as in efforts to separate from her influence, is seen as the same as destroying mother and, as such, is equated with the death of the satellite too. Some years after Robert Corney and I published our paper on the satellite state Heinz Kohut reported similar satellite dreams as part of narcissistic transference (Kohut, 1971). He saw the narcissistic patient's failure to shoot into space from the orbit as a protection against psychosis. He also saw the effective pull to the centre as the narcissistic transference. Kohut's perceptions supplement what Corney and I described earlier and, I think, do not nullify our interpretation of these dreams from the separation–individuation as well as object relation points of view

(Volkan, 1976). Much later another psychoanalyst, Salman Akhtar, who did his psychiatric residency training at the University of Virginia when I was a faculty member there, extended our understanding of clinical manifestations of disturbed optimal distance (Akhtar, 1992a, 1992b).

For a dozen years after his therapy-proper ended, Attis continued "to brush" me or my office at my new location with his "wing". Now, our relationship began to include elements of a father transference. We returned to the state of his condition as it existed at the end of the five years of once-a-week treatment when I moved to a new location: his trying to find a "good" father who could pull him out of his troublesome relationship with his early mother. The following is a description of some events prior to his development of a steady father transference.

He still had his "finger in a bottle" but now he kept it in the attic rather than in his bedroom, and it had lost most of its magic. For years now he showed no preoccupation with it. His vacillation between dependency upon and hostility towards his wife was no longer so marked, and her vagina was no longer perceived as the mouth of a walrus. Attis was not experiencing any hallucinations. During his infrequent visits with me he only had a single repeating symptom: his relationship with a "bitch". Attis was transferred from one church to another in the usual way, remaining at each for an average of three years. In every congregation, he located an older "bad" woman, a "bitch". His appreciation of what she represented did not keep him from experiencing her as the early mother. However, there were no fusions of these "bitches" with the images or representation of his mother or with the images or representation of himself. He knew they stood for his early mother; they were *symbols* of his early mother.

Whenever he came to Charlottesville I saw him for only fifty minutes and handled his sessions in the same way I had conducted his therapy hours when we were working once a week. I continued to charge him for his visits. By the way, throughout his work with me he never paid me directly. When I was in North Carolina he sent his checks to the University of North Carolina's Memorial Hospital. When he saw me in Charlottesville he wrote checks for the University of Virginia Hospital. Physicians who worked at these two university hospitals would only receive salaries; patients' payments would go the hospitals.

Attis began filling his sessions with talk about the "bitches". He was afraid of them, but I noticed that he was also fighting bravely against them. His "fights" with them would range from Attis not answering the "bitches'" questions during church gatherings, to raising his voice when speaking to them, or even, at one time, becoming involved in a "plot" with others who did not like a particular "bitch" in order to remove her from church membership. If he developed extreme anxiety, he would either tolerate it, or make an appointment to come to see me. On one or two occasions during the year, if his fear was too much and he could not wait to drive to Charlottesville, he would call and tell me about his fear of a "bitch". His telephone calls were short, lasting only five or ten minutes. After describing an encounter with a "bitch", he would usually himself declare how she stood for his early "bad" mother. In spite of knowing this, he had anxiety. Calling me briefly and telling his story would help him to relax. Even though we were not in a routine therapy process, I continued to refrain from giving him any advice, but joined him in looking at intrapsychic processes. His "fights" with these older women were his basic psychic exercises in his attempts to complete his separation–individuation phase. In his involvement in these exercises, more and more he saw me as the strong father with whose functions he wished to have more identification. In his sessions I would hear no remarks about my being a "weak" or sadistic father, a "Terrible Turk". He told me that he was reading about Turkey in newspapers and magazines. He hinted that I was a benign Turk.

For the first two years after I became an instructor at the University of Virginia's medical school I had a very small office without windows. Perhaps it was the worst office in the whole university hospital system. Later, as I moved up the professional ladder, I had better offices. I became a stronger father figure for Attis after I moved to an office with windows and after he noticed, while he was waiting in the waiting room, how a secretary talked to me with "respect" when she called to notify me that Attis had come for his session. As I became a stronger father figure in Attis' mind, he became more successful in his fights against "bitches". At that time I was not aware that Attis was teaching me another therapeutic concept, which later I would name "therapeutic play" (Volkan, 1987, 2004b, 2010; Volkan & Ast, 2001; Volkan, Ast & Greer, 2002). Finding "bitches" and "fighting" with them was Attis' therapeutic play.

Therapeutic play refers to patients' certain *actions* inside and/or outside the analyst's office; these actions express an intrapsychic story. They last for some time—weeks, months, even, as Attis' case illustrates, years. Such actions can be considered as two *interrelated* types. One is the repetition through activities of a childhood trauma in order to create the disturbing event in a symbolic fashion in the eternal world while including the mental image of the analyst in the repeated story as a new and helpful object, and then slowly reaching to a new and more adaptive ending of what had been repeated in action. This shows how the individual masters the trauma. And the other type of action is the repetition of a childhood actualised unconscious fantasy, which is related to the trauma, in activities, making the actualised unconscious fantasy conscious *in action* and changing its disturbing influence on the patient. We can consider adult patients involved in a therapeutic play as children playing with toys in an analytic session where their repeating play can be brought under therapeutic scrutiny. Here is an example of an adult's therapeutic play:

In Chapter Four I referred to Gitta who was traumatised by forty surgical interventions beginning in infancy and lasting until she was nineteen years old, and who had an actualised unconscious fantasy of having a leaking body. Unlike Attis who was seeing me very infrequently, Gitta was in analysis with Dr. Gabriele Ast. Renovating her apartment during the second year of her analysis, a process that took a little over nine months, became a crucial part of Gitta's analysis. The apartment represented her leaking body: as she modified its internal structures, repaired its leaking windows, and made it beautiful, she also restructured her mental image of her body and separated what belonged to her "memory" and past feeling states from what was real now. Significantly, her actions incorporated her analyst's image as well. Rather than buying the necessary equipment or material for her work all at once or in substantial instalments, Gitta habitually brought to her sessions a small brush, or a small amount of paint, or some other small item for the renovation that she had purchased on the way to the analyst's office. Dr. Gabriele Ast—who herself enjoys woodworking—would then talk with Gitta about what the patient planned to do to her apartment next, instead of interpreting away the meaning of the patient's action. After the function of repairing her apartment/body image took its course, then the interpretation of the function could be made explicit. In fact, though, doing so was rather unnecessary; by the time Gitta finished renovating, she herself already knew the meaning of her activities. It was the function of her activities that had to be protected until it could serve its purpose. After months of work on the apartment, Gitta could differentiate internally between what belonged to her own mental image of her body and what belonged to the physical existence of the apartment. (Volkan & Ast, 2001)

Attis' therapeutic play lasted for many years. I think that if I had seen him every week or more often, his play would have come to an end much sooner. By then, I had had experiences with other patients who performed therapeutic play, and their involvement in such activities all took place at a faster pace. I will now recount how Attis' therapeutic play ended, first by talking about changes that were happening in my life and then how my patient had noticed these changes. His noticing "improvements" in my life provided a good model for improvements in his.

In 1963 when I moved to Charlottesville and was using an office without windows, horrible things were happening to my family and friends in Cyprus. The British rule ended on the island in 1960 and the Republic of Cyprus was established. But soon ethnic troubles between Cypriot Greeks and Cypriot Turks became inflamed and the Turkish population on the island was forced to live in enclaves surrounded by Cypriot Greek troops. In 1964, United Nations soldiers came to the island and their presence still continues. Cypriot Turks were "imprisoned" from 1963 to 1974 under subhuman conditions in areas that comprised only three per cent of the island. Perhaps my not challenging my assignment of a small windowless office and feeling like I was in a prison had something to do with my identification with my imprisoned family members and friends in Cyprus. In 1968, over eleven years after I had arrived in the United States, I was able to go to the island and visit my family and friends. I noticed that Cypriot Turks in the Nicosia enclave where my parents and sisters were located were raising thousands of parakeets, birds not native to the island, in cages in their run-down homes, in grocery stores, everywhere. Interviewing many people in the Nicosia enclave, I realised that birds in cages represented their imprisoned selves. As long as the birds had babies, survived, and sang, the Cypriot Turks were able, unconsciously, to maintain hope that they would not disappear and one day they would be saved (Volkan, 1979b). After I returned to the United States I could no longer hide my guilt feelings for living in safety while my people were suffering so much and while no one in my surroundings in Charlottesville—and, it seemed, the world—knew about their incredibly tragic situation. My mental condition, I think defensively, made me devote more time to studying psychoanalysis, developing a stronger psychoanalytic identity, and being a better teacher. After moving to Charlottesville I had begun my psychoanalytic training at the Washington Psychoanalytic Institute in Washington, DC. By 1974 I was an instructor at this institute and later I functioned there as a training and supervising analyst.

The Turkish Army went to Cyprus in 1974 and divided the island into Northern Turkish and Southern Greek sections. Greek Cypriots who had homes in the northern part of the island had to flee to the south, leaving their properties behind. This time they suffered more than the Cypriot Turks did. During the war, Cypriot Turks living in the south of the island escaped to the north and were settled in the emptied Greek homes. In 1971 I had become a professor of psychiatry at the University of Virginia, and about the time that the war on Cyprus ended, I took a sabbatical and spent more than a year in Ankara at my old medical school as a visiting professor. I told Attis that I would not be in the United States for thirteen months.

After arriving in Ankara I took the first civilian plane that went to North Cyprus. This time my family members were free to move around in North Cyprus. Those who were still children had not seen the sea because they had been "imprisoned" all their lives in the Nicosia enclave, even though the nearest seashore was only about fifteen miles away. One of my most vivid memories of this visit is noticing the excitement of my sisters' children when we took them to see what the sea looks like. During my sabbatical the ethnic excitement in Turkey for saving the Cypriot Turks from living in enclaves was palpable. I do not remember thinking about Attis much nor communicating with him during the thirteen months when I was enjoying my sabbatical teaching at my old medical school.

On my first visit to my office when I returned to the United States, I noticed a small piece of pink paper on my otherwise empty desk. It said I had just been appointed as the acting chairperson of the Department of Psychiatry. One year later I moved up and became the medical director of the university's newly acquired 600-bed Blue Ridge Hospital, located very near Thomas Jefferson's Monticello. The university's Department of Psychiatry, Department of Orthopedics, some divisions of Internal Medicine and Neurology, some inpatient and outpatient facilities, and laboratories were now located at the Blue Ridge Hospital, which at earlier times had been a hospital for patients with tuberculosis and belonged to the state of Virginia. I would remain as the medical director of the Blue Ridge Hospital for eighteen years and take part in the administration of Virginia University Hospitals in general. Many of the people at Blue Ridge called me "boss", and as the "boss" I had a huge office with a balcony overlooking a beautiful wooded area filled with birds. Starting in 1980 I also became involved in international relations, first taking part in bringing together influential Israelis and Egyptians for unofficial dialogues, which were conducted for six years under the sponsorship of the American Psychiatric Association. Then, in 1989 I created and led the Center for the Study of Mind and Human Interaction at a building on the Blue Ridge Hospital grounds. The Center's multidisciplinary faculty and I would travel to many areas of the world and bring enemy representatives together to tame different international conflicts (Volkan, 2013, 2014b). I also had an office at this Center, but continued to meet with Attis only at my Medical Director's office. Attis was not informed about my involvement in international relations.

Attis came to see me when I was the acting chairperson of the Department of Psychiatry at the main university hospital. He did not complain about the thirteen months I had been unavailable to him. I noted that he had done a great deal of psychological work by himself. I would never learn the details, but I sensed that the months of physical separation between us had caused him to stop being my satellite. A year later he would come to my huge office at Blue Ridge Hospital. While I did not talk with him about changes in my professional life, he could see that I was "moving up". I recall how impressed he was when he first walked into my huge office at Blue Ridge Hospital.

After I returned to Charlottesville from Ankara, Attis told me that he could now say "no" to bitches. He would describe in detail and with glee how he had conquered his fear of "bitches" and how he could put them in their place. But, he continued to talk about them as if it was our routine and habit to discuss this topic. One day while I was in my Blue Ridge Hospital office my telephone rang. Attis was calling. He said, "Oh! There is a new bitch in my church." I guess I spontaneously sensed that he was not anxious, and he was just calling me for a brief contact. I found myself responding, "Oh! Not again!" He burst into laughter. When he stopped laughing, he said, "Thank you," and hung up. The next month he visited me. As soon as he entered my office, with a big smile on his face, he said, "Not again!" From that moment on there were no more "bitches". Attis, no longer my satellite, truly completed his separation–individuation phase. He would continue to visit me several times a year to deal with other psychological issues while climbing up his psychological ladder.

CHAPTER THIRTEEN

Crucial juncture experiences

As Attis stopped "playing" with bitches, I observed his involvement in three new areas. First, his relationship with men, especially when in social settings outside his church, began to change. In the past, he had been guarded with them. For example, at times while playing golf he would wonder if the other men thought of him as a "sissy". Now he felt equal to the other players, and sports competition no longer evoked "I am less than a man" fantasies and anxiety or the psychosomatic symptoms, such as the diarrhoea or stomach-ache, that they once entailed. In fact, Attis began to enjoy men's company. Second, he began to indulge in lively flirtations with various women and even thought of having affairs with them. The third area reflected an intrapsychic change: he could now maintain an integrated self-representation of himself and others. I noticed that he could tolerate ambivalence without returning to utilisation of defensive splitting. I realised that he had gone through *crucial juncture* experiences.

As far as I know, the term "crucial juncture" was first used by Melanie Klein. She wrote: "The synthesis between the loved and hated aspects of the complete object gives rise to the feelings of mourning and guilt which imply vital advances in the infant's emotional and intellectual life. This is also a crucial juncture for the choice of neurosis or psychosis" (Klein, 1946, p. 100). Later, Otto Kernberg and I used this term in describing how patients whose primary defence mechanism is splitting, give up, during their analysis, their dependence on this defence mechanism, and learn how to integrate their self- and object images and representations. Kernberg stated that the pathological narcissistic self-structure (the grandiose self) is resolved in analysis when the patient becomes aware that his ideal concept is basically a fantasy structure. He wrote that "the deep admiration and love for the ideal mother" and "the hatred for the distorted dangerous mother" meet in the transference and, at this crucial point, the patient may experience depression and suicidal thoughts "because he has mistreated the analyst and all the significant persons in his life, and he may feel that he has actually destroyed those whom he could have loved and who might have loved him" (Kernberg, 1970, p. 81). I have described in detail the clinical manifestations of crucial juncture experiences of patients with borderline as well as narcissistic personality organisation in analysis (Volkan, 1974, 1976, 1987, 1993, 1995, 2010, 2014a). During such experiences, none of them became suicidal. I believe this is because these individuals experienced therapeutic regressions before attempting crucial juncture experiences and then had developed stable observing egos. Patients who do not experience such therapeutic regressions and do not develop stable observing egos due to a different technique may be prone to depressions when attempting a crucial juncture experience. I have noticed that some patients, in fact, were delighted to feel for the first time what it is to be "average" in certain life experiences and I also noted their tolerance for ambivalence. One patient spoke about seeing a movie in which a mafia boss first kisses one of his men (he loves him) and the next second he shoots this man (he hates him). The patient said: "When I saw this scene I suddenly understood what it is to put opposite elements together. There were only seconds between the mafia boss showing affection and committing murder. Love and hate touched one another. I realised that I could never do something like that before. I now know why I have been afraid of making grey by mixing black and white. I was afraid of committing murder—getting rid of goodness in me or in others forever. I will try again mixing black and white and this time I hope to make grey."

I cannot report an event in Attis' life illustrating dramatically his sensing and feeling an integrated self-representation and integrated object representations. If he were in regular treatment I suspect that I would have noticed such an event, most likely several of them. What I was noticing was how Attis—then in his mid-fifties, about seventeen years after I first saw him and after he had given up his adaptation to life as a satellite of a central figure or thing—had become a person with a routine high-level personality organisation. He would not refer to events that had dominated his life when he had a psychotic personality organisation. He could remember such events, but since he had developed an ability to repress he would not experience horrible affects that were linked to the events. When a person develops a high-level personality organisation in adulthood he can also, for the first time, experience certain feelings that he had not truly known earlier. He can feel sorrow, remorse, gratitude, and the ability to mourn.

As his identity as an adult male became better established Attis experienced sorrow for not having children and remorse for not having tried to have children. He and Gloria discussed the possibility of adopting children but abandoned it because of his history and their age. Our meetings then were very poignant; he grieved over his childless state and tried to be philosophical about life and the years lost to his psychotic personality organisation and psychotic symptoms. Later, Attis would do his best to be helpful to children and teenagers wherever he lived. He was particularly good with teenagers, understanding them and advising their parents in how to deal with them. He saw in them the sons and daughters he never had.

Mourning in an adult fashion is itself a new experience for patients like Attis and its appearance illustrates a very positive outcome (Searles, 1986). Mourning allows further refinement of reality (Volkan, 1981a); an adult mourner comes to realise that some things or some persons are gone and makes an effort to integrate the experience of loss with reality so life can go on (Pollock, 1989). When the news of Mr. Wiley's death reached him, I noticed that Attis went through genuine grief and mourning. I stood by him while he mourned. Attis could not mourn when he lost his father and then his mother, but his ability to mourn in an adult fashion after losing Mr. Wiley provided further evidence that his psychotic core was gone.

Attis also began looking at oedipal issues for the first time with an integrated self-representation. However, dealing with the oedipal issues at this phase of his life was not like the struggles experienced by persons who in adulthood always had neurotic personality organisation.

When an adult with a neurotic personality organisation comes to analysis, the analytic work deals with the patient's conflicts related to his oedipal issues. On the other hand, Attis, to a great extent, was like a child going through the oedipal phase for the first time with an integrated self-representation, a youngster who was passing through his adolescence passage, expanding his world, and finding new libidinal objects. The technique then needs to be different; the therapist should aim to help the individual like Attis to move up on the developmental ladder.

When he told me about flirting with several women, and sometimes hugging and even kissing them he wondered what I must think of him. In his references to me at this time of his life I was never a representative of his sadistic biological father of his childhood, but a "routine" father figure with whom his son was discussing and exploring an adult male's sexual life. In any case, since I was seeing him infrequently, we were not able to do any serious work on his developmental wishes, activities, and anxieties during his sessions. In his daily life he continued to explore owning his penis. I did not encourage him in his new activities with women, nor did I discourage him. However, when I felt that it was appropriate, I told him that he was like a teenager trying to date for the first time. He was, in his actions, expressing and experiencing his developmental push. He was concerned about what Gloria would say or do if she knew about his flirting with other women. When I listened to him I also noticed that Gloria was no longer a representative of his early mother. She was his wife who had turned into a very close female friend. But, Attis was not having the intense sexual excitement when he was with Gloria that he was experiencing when he was with some other women. Attis genuinely did not wish to hurt Gloria's feelings or to embarrass her. Usually Gloria would accompany him when he drove directly from their home to Charlottesville. Now this routine had changed. They would take a few days of vacation and spend a night at a tourist destination on their way to Charlottesville and another night before returning to their home. After his sessions with me I sometimes noticed how Attis would grasp Gloria's hand in the waiting room and both of them would walk out holding hands as best friends. While relating to some women with whom he had flirted, he was also getting to know more about what ambivalence means. When he noticed a woman with whom he had flirted behaving seductively towards another man,

Attis would feel ambivalence; the woman would remain the same person whom he liked sometimes and who also disappointed him.

Attis developed a more solid confidence in me. He began to experience, first with some shyness and anxiety, something that he was not capable of experiencing before. He tried to be humorous. He tried some jokes on me, which spontaneously amused me. At times, I could see oedipal themes in his jokes. I refrained from interpreting them since I felt that the dominant meaning of telling me jokes was his attempt to have a man-to-man relationship with me and move up on his psychological developmental steps.

During one visit Attis informed me that he had become the lover of a married woman, after a courtship. Both were very careful to be discreet. Linda was a few years younger than him. She was unhappily married to a man who drank a great deal and they had no children. In his sixties, Attis reported happiness he had never before experienced and sexual freedom he had never before known. I made no distinction between Attis' reports of extramarital and other activities. I was as curious about the meaning of his affair as I was about the meaning of his other activities. When I felt it was appropriate, I told Attis that he had made a new adjustment to life in accordance with the new growth in his psychic system; his wife, in the past, symbolised his mother, but he had internally separated from the mother/wife representation and found his own woman, but one who was married to another man. Thus, he still had to work through issues about the reality that he and Linda were married to other individuals, and about triangular or multi-person relationships. I suggested that he would look out for new possibilities, for newer adjustments.

Attis decided to continue with his affair since he felt he had missed a loving and sexually very exciting relationship with a woman all his life. He added: "A man is entitled to fall in love and experience wonderful sexual activity. Now, at last, I have become a man. I will die knowing that, after all, I have received what I was entitled to." He also explained to me that he was also a friend of his lover, who was apparently an intelligent person and who had had a horrible marriage. Furthermore, he informed me that, in spite of his love affair, the friendship between him and Gloria had deepened too.

Attis retired and he and Gloria moved to a new town and bought a house in a nice neighbourhood. About a week after moving there

Attis called me and asked for an appointment. I recalled how the last time he had seen me he had told me that he was not planning to come to Charlottesville until he and Gloria were settled in their new location. He stated that they would be too busy. When he called me for an appointment I wondered what the urgency was. When he came to see me I heard about it right away. Attis told me that he had taken the finger in the bottle to their house, but once there, he had had difficulty knowing where to put it. "I put it in the attic, then in the basement, then in a trunk," he said and added, "I had not thought about it for a long time before our move to a new house. Now, not finding a place for *this thing* bothers me." He looked at me and waited for me to respond. I still recall repeating his words, "this thing" and not saying anything else. He also stayed silent, then smiled and talked about the beauty of their new location, the golf course, and their new neighbours. He came to see me again after three months or so. As soon as he sat in front of me he informed me, casually, as if it was not a big event, that after returning to their new home from our previous session he had thrown the finger in the bottle into a trash can, then the garbage man had taken it away. He did not dwell on his getting rid of "the thing" and changed the topic. He would never again mention the finger in a bottle.

Attis and Gloria became active members in their new social environment. They were involved in raising funds to help especially troubled children and teenagers. Attis, as far as I could learn, was perceived as a leader for community activities that aimed to help children and teenagers. As well as this, many individuals would come to seek Attis' advice for a variety of personal problems. He also enjoyed playing golf, telling jokes, and appreciated the friendship of many men.

Linda had remained in the town where she and Attis had first met. Attis would find excuses to visit her, but infrequently. Once, Linda's husband became ill and almost died. Another time she was in a near-fatal accident and it took a long time for her to recover. Attis handled these realities of life in a mature way. Meanwhile, he and Gloria were also still "best friends". All indications were that Gloria was enjoying a more relaxed Attis.

Attis was not close to his siblings, but when his parents' farm was sold the brother who was responsible for the amputation of Attis' finger claimed more than his share of the proceeds of its sale. Attis led the rest of the family in taking the case to court, where they prevailed. After his parents' estate was settled, Attis was able to extend a friendly hand to the brother who had cut off his finger and who had pressed his claim, and in time they resumed a relatively friendly relationship. His brother invited him to come to Philadelphia again and visit him and his family. What was most heartwarming for me was that Attis did all these things realistically and without much anxiety. He informed me that during his work with me his journey had taken him through many stations. Perhaps there were more stations ahead if he and I continued to travel together. But he was getting older and he wanted to settle in the place where he was. He was content. Soon, however, the cruelties of life would strike and upset his contentment.

CHAPTER FOURTEEN

Physical illnesses and psychic freedom

Whilst still in his sixties, Attis experienced dizzy spells while playing golf on one occasion, and these occurred again when he was in the kitchen at his home. His decades of experience in investigating his internal world led him to seek a possible psychological cause. He could not come up with a reasonable event initiating his dizzy spells. Then he called me. Attis' searching for a psychological explanation of his dizzy spells made me recall a mental image from many years before of myself on my analyst's couch, analysing away a symptom I was having—regurgitation during sleep that would wake me up. My analyst suggested that this might be caused by a hiatal hernia, which proved to be the case. Remembering this, I suggested to Attis that he have a physical examination. He went to see a neurologist who referred him to a cardiologist. Apparently, Attis told this cardiologist that I was his psychiatrist who had urged him to seek a medical cause for his dizzy spells. Later, the cardiologist called me and told me Attis needed a permanent transvenous pacemaker. He had sick sinus syndrome, which causes a spectrum of bradyarrhythmias and, occasionally, bradyarrhythmias following tachycardia. The cardiologist noted that Attis did not want metal in contact with his skin and wondered if there could be a psychological reason for this aversion. When Attis consulted with me, we noticed that his fear over his physical condition had stimulated a fear from his childhood. He refused the cardiologist's advice because the idea of metal contact with his skin represented the axe that had removed his finger. Attis ended up agreeing to a pacemaker if necessary, but when the cardiologist told him that his heart problem would progress slowly and its advance was unpredictable, he decided not to get one and continued a normal physical existence, playing golf, helping teenagers, and occasionally visiting his lover.

Nine years after first seeing the cardiologist Attis played golf three days in a row during Gloria's absence from home and experienced some chest pains. He went to a hospital, where he had a heart attack and fainted. This necessitated triple bypass surgery to save his life, but he knew nothing of what had happened until it was all over. In his post-surgery mental state, he felt confused and uncertain about whether he was dreaming or hallucinating. He had seen his mother, who opened her arms to him, calling, "Come to me!" This frightened him.

After his triple bypass surgery Gloria had called and informed me about this unexpected development. She had also asked the surgeon to call me, which he did. This is how I learned about Attis' post-surgical mental state and confusion. Three weeks after surgery and after he was discharged from the hospital Attis also called me. This time I deliberately kept him on the phone long enough not only to understand how surgery had evoked memories of the past, but also to stand by him during his frightening experience. He was able to tell me his idea that the assault on his body seemed like a punishment and he remembered seeing "fire" in the recovery room. He said, "I knew it was psychologically motivated. I wouldn't tell anyone," and added, "Everything disturbing from my childhood came back to me." He dreamed of donkeys and of how his father had thrust a stick into the anus of one. He thought that he was punished for his marital infidelity and also recalled playing sex with a cousin as a child for which he might now be punished. While he was in his hospital bed he had a feeling that his mother knew all about his sins. "I sensed my old fusion feelings," he said. "But I did not really merge with her, although I sensed her presence."

Attis was unable to urinate after his operation, and when a nurse, a large woman, laughed at him and called him "the bladder boy", he felt that he was being harassed as he had been as a child, in an intrusive, frustrating environment. When he complained of a full bladder the same nurse screamed at him, "If you say another word, I'll tie you to your bed!" In the past he would have turned such a woman into a "bitch". This time, feeling humiliated, he planned to report the incident to his doctor, telling him that such a woman should not be allowed to practise. But the physician and other nurses were very nice to him, so he decided not to criticise.

I was impressed that Attis was involved in a kind of self-analysis during his post-surgery period. One night, after the shock of surgical trauma and the effects of medication had lessened, Attis re-evaluated what had happened to him in reality, felt depressed, and was able to cry. He felt better on the following day. He received a postcard from Linda, who thought it indiscreet to visit him, and he spoke to her on the telephone after being discharged from the hospital.

Attis called me every few days during the next three weeks as though making progress notes. He steadily improved. "The wound on my chest healed beautifully," he reported, adding, "I guess the surgery was also a psychological wound, and it is healing too." He had many visitors and was delighted to realise how many friends he had. Bad dreams, such as the one of his mother inviting him to join her, disappeared. He did dream that someone was asking him to do construction work for which he was not yet ready. He associated with its manifest content by saying that his recovery was like doing construction work and that he was not physically and psychologically ready to complete it.

He did more and more physical exercise some months after his operation and got out of the house more often, resuming his golf. He called to make an appointment with me. "I have something funny to tell you," he said. He did not tell me what it was until he arrived at my office: he had purchased a light-brown car after his recovery from his triple bypass surgery. When he drove it for the first time, he had a sensation in his cut finger. Then, while driving he began to laugh when he realised that the trauma of his surgery had made him repeat, symbolically, the purchase of the flesh-coloured car. Recalling what I had said about his original flesh-coloured car representing his finger/penis, he told himself, "A car is a car!" He reported greatly enjoying his new car and spoke of having driven to see his lover and talking with her.

It was obvious to both of us that this man—once "Jesus Christ", a would-be murderer, a hermaphrodite monster—had a great capacity for self-observation and for reorganising after the regression that had been forced on him by his surgery, medications, and helplessness in a hospital bed. Once more, Attis was my teacher. He was my first patient to describe to me an individual's psychological response to a major surgical trauma. He taught me how such a trauma can induce regression and make traumas of the past reappear. He now stated that he was just fine. But, I could not help noticing that during this first session with me after his triple bypass surgery he looked much thinner than before. He was now seventy years old.

In a later session with me Attis told me that he had decided to go to the next station after all, which meant saying goodbye to his lover. He was grateful to Linda because she had joined him while he allowed himself, at an advanced age, to experience intense sexual pleasures accompanied by loving feelings. Throughout his stay in the hospital and recovery at home Attis had felt highly appreciative of Gloria's genuine concern for him and felt very close to her. Although she had for some time been willing to be his wife in name only, after his recovery from surgery they had resumed sexual relations. Now Attis was finding sexual union with Gloria comforting. Meanwhile, Linda's husband's health was failing, and she was responsible for and busy with his care. Attis discussed with Linda the termination of their affair. She understood this; they decided to remain friends. Attis reported these developments to me, and I listened but offered no opinion.

Attis continued to see Linda but with less and less frequency over the following years. He felt satisfied that he had obtained intense sexual pleasures to which, as a man, he felt he was entitled. Memories of such experiences gave him self-esteem. He and Linda would talk and share their innermost thoughts and feelings. Attis told me that he understood what intimacy meant. Meanwhile, he had become fonder of observing rituals of companionship with Gloria, reading and walking with her. He would never feel the sexual excitement with Gloria that he had experienced with Linda. He was enjoying a different happiness with Gloria, a woman who, rain or shine, stood by him. Then new events occurred to influence his adjustment to his last station in life.

Attis faced new physical problems. He had skin cancer and cysts, one on his neck and another one on the hand that was missing a finger. These were treated surgically, as he reported rather ironically. The brother who had amputated Attis' finger had surgery as well, for a malignant prostate tumour. Attis drove alone to the Philadelphia area and visited his brother in the hospital on two consecutive days. On the way back he had an impulse to go through Linda's town. He stopped there, they met and this time they had sex. While driving home after being with Linda Attis once more was involved in thinking about the psychological factors of his actions. When he later met with me he described his psychological reason for having sex with Linda.

Attis told me that he dreamed the night after visiting his brother of seeing a man plough a field and cut a sewer line. Awakening, he understood that he was the man who was damaging the sewer lines (his brother's prostate). He uncovered his repressed desire for revenge on the dying brother who had taken his finger. Later, while driving back home from Philadelphia, he had realised that his brother's operation fell on the anniversary of President John F. Kennedy's assassination. Thinking about a father figure's assassination, Attis further realised that he had had an unconscious death wish concerning his brother and father. Then he ended up having sex with Linda. In a sense, I understood that after symbolically "killing" an oedipal rival he could have a woman for himself! But, when Attis continued to talk more about his brother, another meaning of his making love to Linda emerged: he was a man in his own right, and therefore he could have his own woman. Attis told me that when he was visiting his brother he found many members of his family there. They had had time to speak about their childhood. Attis noted that his siblings had largely repressed their childhood memories and traumas, and seemed a rather stereotypical, conventional family. Attis thought that he recalled more than the rest of them about their family. He did not tell this to his siblings. However, internally he felt special; he was someone who possessed a more realistic view of their family's background. Psychologically speaking, he was more grown up. This reinforced his sense of self. But, what made a significant impact on him was receiving a beautiful coat from his brother who had had surgery. This brother who had cut off his finger had never given him anything before. This time Attis felt that his brother, by giving him a beautiful coat, was appreciating Attis as someone who was loved and who was a grown-up man, the true leader of their family. Visiting his brother and being with other siblings had evoked wishes of revenge and guilt, but also feelings of psychic freedom, and of being a man in his own right.

Four months later Attis too faced prostate surgery. He came to see me four days before his operation. In a half serious and half joking way he told me that his feelings of revenge towards his brother might have backfired. His brother was dying because his tumour was malignant and could not be removed completely. He wished to talk with his brother and "tie up loose ends". But, he knew that his brother might not understand human psychology and might be disturbed if his younger brother attempted such a discussion. Attis' tumour was not malignant. He felt luckier than his brother and just before he left my office he joked about paying doctor bills all his life. I knew that he was anxious in spite of his joking.

His prostate surgery was successful. Later I would learn from him that his experience with prostate surgery reminded him of some incidents that had followed his triple bypass surgery. When he woke up in bed, he found that a nurse had tied a blue ribbon on his penis, and he felt humiliated. This time the nurse was not the large woman, but a petite one. Attis did not turn her into a "bitch" either. Instead, when he met with me he connected the petite nurse's action with his childhood mother's lack of empathy for him. Then, with excitement, he went on to tell me his understanding of the unconscious psychological aspects of a wish he had had prior to the prostate surgery. At such times I sensed Attis loved to be a "psychoanalyst", analysing himself. I would simply watch him, listen to him, and appreciate his enjoyment. He had a fantasy of taking a trip with Gloria to the Grand Canyon. He concluded that, "The Grand Canyon is a big vagina." He then added that this wish was connected with his conquering his childhood fear of vaginas. He knew that his fear of this surgery too was stimulating his recollection of his childhood fears. He joked: "At my age, I'm not going walking around the Grand Canyon! It's good to know where this unusual wish comes from."

Going back to his childhood this time gave Attis a new and very significant insight. He recalled a childhood memory of wishing to touch his mother's breast. His mother would not allow it, saying that her aunt had big breasts and he should fondle hers. He remembered awaiting a visit from this aunt, but she too forbade his fondling her breast. Attis now realised that Linda had large breasts, and he wondered if his lover might also represent this aunt in other ways. He wondered if he was creating an aunt/mother who would not reject him but would take him to her bosom and give him pleasure and affirmation instead of a fragile self-representation. He realised that Linda satisfied him not only as a lover, but also as a "good" transference object. He added, "I am glad and proud of myself that I had the opportunity to change the bad things from my childhood into better ones!"

CHAPTER FIFTEEN

Sunset

After his prostate surgery Attis experienced more heart problems. He was still in his early seventies. One morning he woke up with severe chest pains and was taken to a hospital where he underwent further heart surgery, which was minor in comparison to his triple bypass operation. While he was recovering in the hospital, Linda's husband, who had been ailing for some time, died. It was a while before Attis could visit Linda after this, and when he did he found her grieving. He encouraged her to grieve further.

Soon, Attis would give an anguished response to the death of his brother who had cut his finger. He came to tell me that old childhood issues had been appearing in his dreams. After seeing me he drove to the place his brother had lived, accompanied by Gloria. He wanted to visit his brother's widow, but Gloria thought that would not be a good idea since, while Attis and his brother had become friendly after their parents' estate issue was settled, his brother's wife had not been welcoming. Attis and Gloria went to the cemetery where his brother was buried. He walked to his brother's grave alone and prayed for his brother's soul. The next day he called me and told me the dream he had had that night. In the dream Attis was standing in a room with a woman Attis knew was his mother. She opened the door of the room and just walked away. Attis was not only saying goodbye to his brother, his mother's agent, but also to his mother.

During his next visits with me I found his personality organisation better integrated than ever before. At his last visit I told him that I had never seen him so well mentally and upon hearing this he became tearful, as did I. I was worried about his physical wellbeing because he looked pale and tired. He told me how he was taking heart medications and getting old. He and Gloria had driven hundreds of miles to see me and checked in at the same motel where they usually stayed during their visits to Charlottesville. He needed more sleep and told Gloria how difficult it was going to be in the future for him to make the trip to see me. He was still having occasional chest pains. His cardiologist was not sure if these pains were caused by a possible hiatal hernia or whether they were the beginnings of another heart problem. Attis told me that he might not come to see me again, but he would call me. When they left I found myself wondering if I would ever see Attis again. I would not.

Through his infrequent telephone calls I learned that Attis and Gloria sold their house and bought a nice apartment in a resort area on the North Carolina shore. I noted that one reason for their doing so was that his cardiologist had moved there to accept a good position at a new hospital. Attis and Gloria felt safer relocating to where they would have access to the cardiologist whom they trusted. Attis continued to have occasional chest pains throughout the next few years, but whenever he called me he sounded content and relaxed. I still vividly remember his last telephone call to me. He said:

> I am sitting on my balcony and watching the sea. It is so beautiful here. I am with Gloria and we are very happy. By the way (laughter), here too, neighbours, especially teenagers, have been treating me as if I am a psychotherapist. I guess they also know that once upon a time I was a Methodist minister. I do not go out much, but they visit me often and share their problems. Oh, don't worry, I also know how to protect myself. I enjoy helping people, but if I am tired I protect myself. Oh, the sunset last evening was incredible. I love to watch the sun disappearing into the sea. I guess I am thinking of my disappearance. I will disappear like the sun, while feeling shiny and happy. But, you know, unlike the sun I will not reappear the next day.

I never heard from Attis again. He died in his early eighties. My hunch is that Gloria tried to get in touch with me after he died. By then I had retired and she would not have been able to reach me at the university. If she was able to find my home telephone number she still would not have found me as I was out of the country at that time. After not hearing from Attis for a long time I knew that he had died. But, I guess, I wanted to deny it and never checked to learn the circumstances of his death. Only when I decided to write the book, with the aid of the internet, I easily found the date of his death and information about his funeral. One man who spoke at this funeral referred to Attis as a great man who had dedicated himself to his neighbours, teenagers in general, never hesitated to be helpful, and who loved to watch sunsets.

Last words

This book presents the whole life story of an unusual man, Attis, who had learned to examine his inner world. I met him when he was thirty-nine years old. During the first five years of our work together his psychotic core was modified. No medication was ever used. Unfortunately, we could not continue his treatment in order for his psyche to have further drastic structural modifications within the usual pace of treatment. It seems that the first five years of treatment had put him on the right track. Over the next twelve years or so, he adjusted to life according to his modified internal structure. Then, until his death in his early eighties, without any intensive therapeutic work, but by using me and some others as transference figures, he began moving up further on his developmental ladder.

I hope that the case of Attis will stimulate the reader to think about questions regarding the nature of his illness and psychotic personality organisation in general, the role of identification with the therapist, the tolerance of emotional flooding, the influence of real-life events, countertransference, and other related issues. I also hope that several therapeutic concepts described in this book and their clinical illustrations may influence those who are psychoanalytically trained and other mental health professionals, and encourage them not to lose sight of the importance of the psychodynamic approach to individuals like Attis who was not only my patient, but also one of my best teachers. In this book I share with the reader what he taught me.

REFERENCES

Abse, D. W., & Ewing, J. A. (1960). Some problems in psychotherapy with schizophrenic patients. *American Journal of Psychotherapy, 14*: 505–519.

Ainslie, R. C., & Solyom, A. E. (1986). The replacement of the fantasied oedipal child: A disruptive effect of sibling loss on the mother–infant relationship. *Psychoanalytic Psychology, 3*: 257–268.

Akhtar, S. (1992a). Tethers, orbits and invisible fences: Clinical, developmental, sociocultural, and technical aspects of optimal distance. In: S. Kramer & S. Akhtar (Eds.), *When the Body Speaks: Psychological Meanings in Kinetic Clues* (pp. 21–57). Northvale, NJ: Jason Aronson.

Akhtar, S. (1992b). *Broken Structures: Severe Personality Disorders and Their Treatment.* Northvale, NJ: Jason Aronson.

Alanen, Y. O. (1993). *Skitsofrenia: Syyt Tarpeenmukainen Hoito (Schizophrenia and Need-Adapted Treatment).* Juva, Finland: WSOY.

Apprey, M. (1997). The intersubjective constitution of the sense of disappearing in schizophrenia: A phenomenological description of a healthy sibling's intuitions. In: V. D. Volkan & S. Akhtar (Eds.), *The Seed of Madness: Constitution, Environment, and Fantasy* (pp. 81–109). Madison, CT: International Universities Press.

Arlow, J. A. (1969). Unconscious fantasy and disturbances of conscious experience. *Psychoanalytic Quarterly, 38*: 1–27.

135

Beres, D. (1962). The unconscious fantasy. *Psychoanalytic Quarterly, 31*: 309–329.

Bernstein, D. (1990). Female genital anxieties, conflicts, and typical mastery modes. *International Journal of Psychoanalysis, 71*: 151–165.

Beutel, M. E., Stern, E., & Silbersweig, D. A. (2003). The emerging dialogue between psychoanalysis and neuroscience: Neuroimaging perspectives. *Journal of the American Psychoanalytic Association, 51*: 773–801.

Blackman, J. (2014). Fear of injury. In: S. Akhtar (Ed.), *Fear: A Dark Shadow Across our Life Span* (pp. 123–146). London: Karnac.

Bloom, P. (2010). *How Pleasure Works: The New Science of Why We Like What We Like*. New York: W. W. Norton.

Blos, P. (1979). *The Adolescent Passage: Developmental Issues*. New York: International Universities Press.

Bond, D. D. (1952). *The Love and Fear of Flying*. New York: International Universities Press.

Bowlby, J. (1953). Some pathological processes set in train by early mother–child separation. *Journal of Mental Science, 99*: 265–272.

Bowlby, J. (1969). *Attachment*. New York: Basic.

Boyer, L. B. (1961). Provisional evaluation of psycho-analysis with few parameters in the treatment of schizophrenics. *International Journal of Psychoanalysis, 42*: 389–403.

Boyer, L. B. (1967). Office treatment of schizophrenic patients: The use of psychoanalytic therapy with few parameters. In: L. B. Boyer & P. L. Giovacchini (Eds.), *Psychoanalytic Treatment of Characterological and Schizophrenic Patients* (pp. 143–188). New York: Science House.

Boyer, L. B. (1971). Psychoanalytic technique in the treatment of certain characterological and schizophrenic disorders. *International Journal of Psychoanalysis, 52*: 67–85.

Boyer, L. B. (1983). *The Regressed Patient*. New York: Jason Aronson.

Brazelton, T. B., & Greenspan, S. I. (2000). *The Irreducible Needs of Children: What Every Child Must Have to Grow, Learn and Flourish*. Cambridge, MA: Perseus.

Brenner, I. (2001). *Dissociation of Trauma: Theory, Phenomenology, and Technique*. Madison, CT: International Universities Press.

Brenner, I. (2004). *Psychic Trauma: Dynamics, Symptoms, and Treatment*. New York: Jason Aronson.

Burnham, D. L. (1969). Schizophrenia and object relations. In: D. L. Burnham, A. I. Gladstone, & R. W. Gibson (Eds.), *Schizophrenia and the Need-Fear Dilemma* (pp. 15–41). New York: International Universities Press.

Cain, A. C., & Cain, B. S. (1964). On replacing a child. *Journal of the American Academy of Child Psychiatry, 3*: 443–456.

Cameron, N. (1961). Introjection, reprojection, and hallucination in the interaction between schizophrenic patients and the therapist. *International Journal of Psychoanalysis, 42*: 86–96.

Cancro, R. (1986). General considerations relating to theory in schizophrenic disorders. In: D. B. Finesilver (Ed.), *Towards a Comprehensive Model for Schizophrenic Disorders* (pp. 97–107). New York: Analytic.

Comert, P. (2006). Becoming a murderer without committing murder: Unconscious murder fantasies in sibling relationships. Paper presented at the Division 39 of the American Psychological Association Conference, April 19–23, Philadelphia, PA.

Cortés, L. (1978). *Un Enigma Salmantino: La Rana Universitaria*. Salamanca, Spain: Gráficas Cervantes.

Dorpat, T. L. (1976). Structural conflict and object relations conflict. *Journal of the American Psychoanalytic Association, 24*: 855–874.

Dorpat, T. L. (2002). *Wounded Monster: Hitler's Path from Trauma to Malevolence*. New York: University Press of America.

Duncan, C. (2002). *Psychoanalysis, Violence and Rage-Type Murder: Murdering Minds*. New York: Routledge.

Eissler, K. R. (1954). Notes upon defects of ego structure in schizophrenia. *International Journal of Psychoanalysis, 35*: 141–146.

Ekstein, R. N. (1966). *Children of Time and Space, of Action and Impulse: Clinical Studies on the Psychoanalytic Treatment of Severely Disturbed Children*. East Norwalk, CT: Appleton-Century Crofts.

Emde, R. N. (1991). Positive emotions for psychoanalytic theory: Surprises from infancy research and new directions. *Journal of the American Psychoanalytic Association* (Supplement), *39*: 5–44.

Faimberg, H. (2005). *The Telescoping of Generations: Listening to the Narcissistic Links Between Generations*. London: Routledge.

Fenichel, O. (1945). *The Psychoanalytic Theory of Neurosis*. New York: W. W. Norton.

Ferenczi, S. (1909). *First Contributions to Psychoanalysis*. London: Hogarth, 1952.

Fonagy, P. (2001). The psychoanalysis of violence. Paper presented at Dallas Society for Psychoanalytic Psychology seminar Preventing Mass Murder in Schools: Understanding Violent Children from "Peaceful" Families, 15 March, Dallas, TX.

Fonagy, P., & Target, M. (1996). Playing with reality I: Theory of mind and the normal development of psychic reality. *International Journal of Psychoanalysis, 77*: 217–233.

Fonagy, P., & Target, M. (1997). Attachment and reflective function: Their role in self-organisation. *Development and Psychopathology, 9*: 679–700.

Fonagy, P., & Target, M. (2002). Understanding the violent patient: The use of the body and the role of the father. *Kinderanalyse, 10*: 280–307.

Freeman, T. (1983). Reexamining schizophrenia. *Psychoanalytic Inquiry, 3*: 71–89.

Freud, A. (1936). *The Ego and the Mechanism of Defense*. New York: International Universities Press, 1946.

Freud, A. (1954). The widening scope of indications for psychoanalysis. In: *The Writings of Anna Freud, Volume 4* (pp. 356–376). New York: International Universities Press, 1968.

Freud, A. (1968). *The Writings of Anna Freud, Volumes 1–4*. New York: International Universities Press.

Freud, S. (1887–1902). *The Origins of Psycho-Analysis: Letters to Wilhelm Fliess, Drafts and Notes* (Ed. M. Bonaparte, A. Freud & E. Krist). New York: Basic, 1954.

Freud, S. (1900a). *The Interpretation of Dreams*. S.E., 4–5. London: Hogarth.

Freud, S. (1905d). Three essays on the theory of sexuality. *S.E., 7*: 130–242. London: Hogarth.

Freud, S. (1908a). On hysterical phantasies and their relation to bisexuality. *S.E., 9*: 155–166. London: Hogarth.

Freud, S. (1916–1917). *Introductory Lectures on Psychoanalysis. S.E., 16*. London: Hogarth.

Freud, S. (1917e). Mourning and melancholia. *S.E., 14*: 237–258. London: Hogarth.

Freud, S. (1919h). The "uncanny". *S.E., 17*: 217–252. London: Hogarth.

Freud, S. (1920g). Beyond the pleasure principle. *S.E., 18*: 7–64. London: Hogarth.

Fromm-Reichmann, F. (1959). *Psychoanalysis and Psychotherapy*. Chicago: Chicago University Press.

Gedo, J. E. (1979). *Beyond Interpretation: Toward a Revised Theory for Psychoanalysis*. New York: International Universities Press.

Giovacchini, P. L. (1969). The influence of interpretation upon schizophrenic patients. *International Journal of Psychoanalysis, 50*: 179–186.

Giovacchini, P. L. (1972). Interpretation and the definition of the analytic setting. In: *Tactics and Techniques in Psychoanalytic Therapy, Volume 2*, (pp. 5–94). New York: Jason Aronson.

Glass, J. (1985). *Delusion: Internal Dimensions of Political Life*. Chicago: Chicago University Press.

Graves, R. (1957). *The Greek Myths*. New York: George Braziller.

Green, N., & Solnit, A. J. (1964). Reactions to the threatened loss of a child: A vulnerable child syndrome. *Pediatrics, 34*: 58–66.

Greenspan, S. I. (1989). *The Development of the Ego: Implications for Personality Theory, Psychopathology and the Psychotherapeutic Process*. Madison, CT: International Universities Press.

Greenspan, S. I. (1997). *The Growth of the Mind and the Endangered Origins of Intelligence*. Cambridge, MA: Perseus.

Heimann, P. (1956). Dynamics of transference interpretations. *International Journal of Psychoanalysis, 37*: 303–310.

Hoedemaker, E. D. (1955). The therapeutic process in the treatment of schizophrenia. *Journal of the American Psychoanalytic Association, 3*: 89–109.

Inderbitzin, L. B., & Levy, S. T. (1990). Unconscious fantasy: A reconsideration of the concept. *Journal of the American Psychoanalytic Association, 38*: 113–130.

Jacobson, E. (1954). Transference problems in the psychoanalytic treatment of severely depressive patients. *Journal of the American Psychoanalytic Association, 2*: 595–606.

Jacobson, E. (1964). *The Self and the Object World*. New York: International Universities Press.

Kerényi, C. (1980). *Gods of the Greeks*. New York: Thames & Hudson.

Kernberg, O. F. (1966). Structural derivatives of object relationships. *International Journal of Psychoanalysis, 47*: 236–253.

Kernberg, O. F. (1969). A contribution to the ego-psychological critique of the Kleinian school. *International Journal of Psychoanalysis, 50*: 317–333.

Kernberg, O. F. (1970). Factors in the psychoanalytic treatment of narcissistic personalities. *Journal of the American Psychoanalytic Association, 18*: 51–85.

Kernberg, O. F. (1975). *Borderline Conditions and Pathological Narcissism*. New York: Jason Aronson.

Kernberg, O. F. (1976). *Object Relations Theory and Clinical Psychoanalysis*. New York: Jason Aronson.

Kernberg, O. F. (1980). *Internal World and External Reality: Object Relations Theory Applied*. New York: Jason Aronson.

Kernberg, O. F. (1988). Object relations theory in clinical practice. *Psychoanalytic Quarterly, 57*: 481–504.

Kestenberg, J. S. (1982). A psychological assessment based on analysis of a survivor's child. In: M. S. Bergman & M. E. Jucovy (Eds.), *Generations of the Holocaust* (pp. 158–177). New York: Columbia University Press.

Klein, M. (1946). Notes on some schizoid mechanisms. *International Journal of Psychoanalysis, 27*: 99–110.

Klein, M. (1948). *Contributions to Psychoanalysis, 1921–1945*. London: Hogarth.

Kohut, H. (1971). *The Analysis of the Self: A Systematic Approach to the Psychoanalytic Treatment of Narcissistic Personality Disorders*. New York: International Universities Press.

Langer, W. C. (1972). *The Mind of Hitler: The Secret Wartime Report*. New York: Basic.

Laufer, E. (Ed.) (2013). *On the Frontiers of Psychoanalysis and Neuroscience: Essays in Honor of Eric R. Kandel*. New York: Guilford.

Legg, C., & Sherick, I. (1976). The replacement child—a developmental tragedy: Some preliminary comments. *Child Psychiatry and Human Development, 7*: 79–97.

Lehtonen, J. (2003). The dream between neuroscience and psychoanalysis: Has feeding an infant an impact on brain function and the capacity to create dream images in infants? *Psychoanalysis in Europe, 57*: 175–182.

Leigh, H., & Reiser, M. F. (1992). *The Patient: Biological, Psychological, and Social Dimensions of Medical Practice* (3rd edition). New York: Plenum Medical.

Levin, B. D. (1935). Claustrophobia. *Psychoanalytic Quarterly, 4*: 227–233.

Levin, F. M. (2004). *Psyche and Brain: The Biology of Talking Cure*. Guilford, CT: International Universities Press.

Limentani, D. (1956). Symbiotic identification in schizophrenia. *Psychiatry, 19*: 231–236.

Loewald, H. W. (1960). On the therapeutic action of psychoanalysis. *International Journal of Psychoanalysis, 41*: 16–33.

Mahler, M. S. (1968). *On Human Symbiosis and the Vicissitudes of Individuation*. New York: International Universities Press.

Mahler, M. S., & Furer, M. (1963). Certain aspects of the separation–individuation phase. *Psychoanalytic Quarterly, 32*: 1–14.

Mahler, M. S., & Furer, M. (1966). Development of symbiosis, symbiotic psychoses, and the nature of separation anxiety: Remarks on Welland's paper. *International Journal of Psychoanalysis, 47*: 559–560.

Mahler, M. S., Pine, F., & Bergman, A. (1975). *The Psychological Birth of the Human Infant*. New York: Basic.

Modell, A. H. (1975). A narcissistic defence against affects and the illusion of self-sufficiency. *International Journal of Psychoanalysis, 56*: 275–282.

Niederland, W. G. (1968). Clinical observations on the "survivor syndrome". *International Journal of Psychoanalysis, 49*: 313–315.

Novey, S. (1968). *The Second Look: The Reconstruction of Personal History in Psychiatry and Psychoanalysis*. Baltimore, MD: Johns Hopkins.

Olinick, S. L. (1980). *The Psychotherapeutic Instrument*. New York: Jason Aronson.

Olsson, P. A. (2014). *The Making of a Homegrown Terrorist: Brainwashing Rebels in Search of a Cause*. Santa Barbara, CA: ABC-CLIO/Praege.

Öztürk, O., & Volkan, V. D. (1971). The theory and practice of psychiatry in Turkey. *American Journal of Psychotherapy, 25*: 240–271.

Pao, P. -N. (1979). *Schizophrenic Disorders: Theory and Treatment from a Psychodynamic Point of View*. New York: International Universities Press.

Parens, H. (1979). *The Development of Aggression in Early Childhood*. New York: Jason Aronson. [Revised edition Lanham, MD: Rowman & Littlefield, 2008].

Parens, H. (2007). Roots of prejudice: Findings from observational research. In: H. Parens, A. Mahfouz, S. Twemlow & D. Scharff (Eds.), *The Future of Prejudice: Psychoanalysis and the Prevention of Prejudice* (pp. 81–95). New York: Rowman & Littlefield.

Peto, A. (1968). On affect control. *International Journal of Psychoanalysis, 49*: 471–473.

Pollock, G. (1989). *The Mourning-Liberation Process, Volumes 1 and 2*. Madison, CT: International Universities Press.

Poznanski, E. O. (1972). The "replacement child": A saga of unresolved parental grief. *Behavioral Pediatrics, 81*: 1190–1193.

Purhonen, M., Pääkkönen, A., Yppärilä, H., Lehtonen, J., & Karhu, J. (2001). Dynamic behaviour of the auditory N100 elicited by a baby's cry. *International Journal of Psychophysiology, 41*: 271–278.

Rapaport, D. (1951). *Organization and Pathology of Thought: Selected Papers*. New York: Columbia University Press.

Reiser, M. F. (1990). *Memory in Mind and Brain*. New York: Basic.

Rosenfeld, D. (1992). *The Psychotic: Aspects of the Personality*. London: Karnac.

Rosenfeld, H. A. (1965). *Psychotic States: A Psychoanalytic Approach*. London: Hogarth.

Rudden, M. G. (2011). The "secret cocoon": Fantasies about the private self in the absence of consensual reality. *International Journal of Psychoanalysis, 92*: 359–376.

Sandler, J., & Nagera, H. (1963). Aspects of metapsychology of fantasy. *The Psychoanalytic Study of the Child, 18*: 159–194.

Schützenberger, A. A. (1998). *The Ancestor Syndrome: Transgenerational Psychotherapy and the Hidden Links in the Family Tree* (Trans. A. Trager). New York: Routledge.

Searles, H. F. (1951). Data concerning certain manifestations of incorporation. *Psychiatry, 14*: 397–413.

Searles, H. F. (1986). *My Work with Borderline Patients*. Northvale, NJ: Aronson.

Sechehaye, M. A. (1951). *Symbolic Realisation*. New York: International Universities Press.

Shapiro, T. (1990). Unconscious fantasy: Introduction. *Journal of the American Psychoanalytic Association, 37*: 38–46.

Shapiro, T. (2008). Masturbation, sexuality, and adaptation: Normalization in adolescence. *Journal of the American Psychoanalytic Association, 56*: 123–146.

Shengold, L. (1991). *Soul Murder: The Effects of Childhood Abuse and Deprivation.* New York: Ballantine.

Silverman, L. H. (1979). Two unconscious fantasies as mediators of successful psychotherapy. *Psychotherapy, 16*: 215–230.

Solms, M., & Turnbull, O. (2010). *The Brain and the Inner World: An Introduction to the Neuroscience of Subjective Experience.* New York: Other.

Spitz, R. A. (1946). The smiling response: A contribution to the ontogenesis of social relations. *Genetic Psychology Monographs, 34*: 57–125.

Spitz, R. A. (1965). *The First Year of Life: A Psychoanalytic Study of Normal and Deviant Development of Object Relations.* New York: International Universities Press.

Stern, D. N. (1985). *The Interpersonal World of the Infant.* New York: Basic.

Stone, L. (1954). The widening scope of indications for psychoanalysis. *Journal of the American Psychoanalytic Association, 2*: 567–594.

Stone, M. H. (1989). Murder: Narcissistic personality disorder. *Psychiatric Clinics of North America, 12*: 643–651.

Stone, M. H. (2009). *The Anatomy of Evil.* Amherst, NY: Prometheus.

Strachey, J. (1934). The nature of the therapeutic action of psychoanalysis. *International Journal of Psychoanalysis, 15*: 127–159.

Sullivan, H. S. (1962). *Schizophrenia as a Human Process.* New York: W. W. Norton.

Szasz, T. S. (1957). A contribution to the psychology of schizophrenia. *Archives of Neurology and Psychiatry, 77*: 420–436.

Tähkä, V. (1984). Dealing with object loss. *Scandinavian Psychoanalytic Review, 7*: 13–33.

Tähkä, V. (1993). *Mind and Its Treatment: A Psychoanalytic Approach.* Madison, CT: International Universities Press.

Target, M., & Fonagy, P. (1996). Playing with reality I: Theory of mind and the normal development of psychic reality. *International Journal of Psychoanalysis, 77*: 459–479.

Tienari, P. (1991). Interaction between genetic vulnerability and family environment: The Finnish adoptive family study of schizophrenia. *Acta Psychaitrica Scandinavica, 84*: 460–465.

Tizón, L. J. (2007). Psicoanalisis, procesos de duelo y psicosis (Psychoanalysis, Mourning Processes, and Psychosis). Barcelona: Herder-PPP.

Torsti, M. (1998). On motherhood. *Scandinavian Psychoanalytic Review, 21*: 53–76.

Van der Kolk, B. (2000). Trauma, neuroscience, and the etiology of hysteria: An exploration of the relevance of Breuer and Freud's 1893 article in light of modern science. *Journal of the American Psychoanalytic Association, 28*: 237–262.

Volkan, V. D. (1973). Transitional fantasies in the analysis of a narcissistic personality. *Journal of the American Psychoanalytic Association, 21*: 351–376.

Volkan, V. D. (1974). Cosmic laughter: A study of primitive splitting. In: P. C. Giovacchini, A. Flarsheim & L. B. Boyer (Eds.), *Tactics and Technique of Psychoanalytic Psychotherapy, Volume 2* (pp. 425–440). New York: Jason Aronson.

Volkan, V. D. (1976). *Primitive Internalized Object Relations: A Clinical Study of Schizophrenic, Borderline and Narcissistic Patients*. New York: International Universities Press.

Volkan, V. D. (1979a). The glass bubble of a narcissistic patient. In: J. LeBoit & A. Capponi (Eds.), *Advances in Psychotherapy of the Borderline Patient* (pp. 405–431). New York: Jason Aronson.

Volkan, V. D. (1979b). *Cyprus-War and Adaptation: A Psychoanalytic History of Two Ethnic Groups in Conflict*. Charlottesville, VA: University of Virginia Press.

Volkan, V. D. (1981a). *Linking Objects and Linking Phenomena: A Study of the Forms, Symptoms, Metapsychology and Therapy of Complicated Mourning*. New York: International Universities Press.

Volkan, V. D. (1981b). Transference and countertransference: An examination from the point of view of internalised object relations. In: S. Tuttman, C. Kaye & M. Zimmerman (Eds.), *Object and Self: A Developmental Approach (Essays in Honor of Edith Jacobson)* (pp. 429–451). New York: International Universities Press.

Volkan, V. D. (1985). Becoming a psychoanalyst. In: J. Reppen (Ed.), *Analysts at Work: Practice, Principles and Techniques* (pp. 215–231). Hillsdale, NJ: Analytic.

Volkan, V. D. (1987). *Six Steps in the Treatment of Borderline Personality Organization*. Northvale, NJ: Jason Aronson.

Volkan, V. D. (1988). *The Need to Have Enemies and Allies: From Clinical Practice to International Relationships*. Northvale, NJ: Jason Aronson.

Volkan, V. D. (1993). Countertransference reactions commonly present in the treatment of patients with borderline personality organisation. In: A. Alexandris & C. Vaslamatis (Eds.), *Countertransference and How it Effects the Interpretive Work* (pp. 147–163). London: Karnac.

Volkan, V. D. (1995). *The Infantile Psychotic Self: Understanding and Treating Schizophrenics and Other Difficult Patients*. Northvale, NJ: Jason Aronson.

Volkan, V. D. (1997). *Bloodlines: From Ethnic Pride to Ethnic Terrorism*. New York: Farrar, Straus and Giroux.

Volkan, V. D. (2004a). *Blind Trust: Large Groups and Their Leaders in Times of Crisis and Terror*. Charlottesville, VA: Pitchstone.

Volkan, V. D. (2004b). Actualised unconscious fantasies and "therapeutic play" in adults' analyses: Further study of these concepts. In: A. Laine (Ed.), *Power of Understanding: Essays in Honour of Veikko Tähkä* (pp. 119–141). London: Karnac.

Volkan, V. D. (2006). *Killing in the Name of Identity: A Study of Bloody Conflicts*. Charlottesville, VA: Pitchstone.

Volkan, V. D. (2007a). Individuals and societies as "perennial mourners": Their linking objects and public memorials. In: B. Wilcock, L. C. Bohm & R. Curtis (Eds.), *On Death and Endings: Psychoanalysts' Reflections on Finality, Transformations and New Beginnings* (pp. 42–59). Philadelphia, PA: Routledge.

Volkan, V. D. (2007b). Not letting go: From individual perennial mourners to societies with entitlement ideologies. In: L. G. Fiorini, S. Lewkowicz & T. Bokanowsky (Eds.), *On Freud's "Mourning and Melancholia"* (pp. 90–109). London: International Psychoanalytic Association.

Volkan, V. D. (2009). The next chapter: Consequences of societal trauma. In: P. Gobodo-Madikizela & C. van der Merwe (Eds.), *Memory, Narrative and Forgiveness: Perspectives of the Unfinished Journeys of the Past* (pp. 1–26). Cambridge: Cambridge Scholars.

Volkan, V. D. (2010). *Psychoanalytic Technique Expanded: A Textbook on Psychoanalytic Treatment*. Istanbul: Oa.

Volkan, V. D. (2013). *Enemies on the Couch: A Psychopolitical Journey through War and Peace*. Durham, NC: Pitchstone.

Volkan, V. D. (2014a). *Animal Killer: Transmission of War Trauma from One Generation to the Next*. London: Karnac.

Volkan, V. D. (2014b). *Psychoanalysis, Internal Relations, and Diplomacy: A Source Book on Large-Group Psychology*. London: Karnac.

Volkan, V. D., & Akhtar, S. (Eds.) (1997). *The Seed of Madness: Constitution, Environment, and Fantasy in the Organisation of the Psychotic Core*. Madison, CT: International Universities Press.

Volkan, V. D., & Ast, G. (1994). *Spektrum des Narzißmus: Eine klinische Studie des gesunden Narzißmus, des narzißtisch-masochistischen Charakters, der narzißtischen Persönlichkeitsorganisation, des malignen Narzißmus und des erfolgreichen Narzißmus. (Spectrum of Narcissism: A Clinical Study of Healthy Narcissism, Narcissistic-Masochistic Character, Narcissistic Personality-Organisation, Malignant Narcissism, and Successful Narcissism)*. Göttingen: Vandenhoeck & Ruprecht.

Volkan, V. D., & Ast, G. (1997). *Siblings in the Unconscious and Psychopathology: Womb Fantasies, Claustrophobias, Fear of Pregnancy, Murderous Rage, Animal Symbolism.* London: Karnac, 2014.

Volkan, V. D., & Ast, G. (2001). Curing Gitta's "leaking body": Actualized unconscious fantasies and therapeutic play. *Journal of Clinical Psychoanalysis, 10*: 567–606.

Volkan, V. D., Ast, G., & Greer, W. F. (2002). *The Third Reich in the Unconscious: Transgenerational Transmission and its Consequences.* New York: Brunner-Routledge.

Volkan, V. D., & Corney, R. T. (1968). Some considerations of satellite states and satellite dreams. *British Journal of Medical Psychology, 41*: 283–290.

Volkan, V. D., & Fowler, C. (2009). *Searching for a Perfect Woman: The Story of a Complete Psychoanalysis.* New York: Jason Aronson.

Volkan, V. D., & Kayatekin, S. (2006). Extreme religious fundamentalism and violence: Some psychoanalytic and psychopolitical thoughts. *Psyche & Geloof, 17*: 71–91.

Volkan, V. D., & Zintl, E. (1993). *Life After Loss: Lessons of Grief.* New York: Charles Scribner's Sons.

Weigert, E. (1938). The cult and mythology of the Magna Mater from the standpoint of psychoanalysis. *Psychiatry, 1*: 347–378.

Weigert, E. (1954). The importance of flexibility in psychoanalytic technique. *Journal of the American Psychoanalytic Association, 2*: 702–710.

Werner, H., & Kaplan, B. (1963). *Symbol Formation.* New York: Wiley.

Winnicott, D. W. (1953). Transitional objects and transitional phenomena. *International Journal of Psychoanalysis, 34*: 89–97.

Winnicott, D. W. (1963). The value of depression. In: C. Winnicott, R. Shepherd & M. Davis (Eds.), *D. W. Winnicott: Home is Where We Start From* (pp. 75–92). New York: W. W. Norton, 1986.

Winnicott, D. W. (1969). Berlin walls. In: C. Winnicott, R. Shepherd, & M. Davis (Eds.), *D. W. Winnicott: Home is Where We Start From* (pp. 221–227). New York: W. W. Norton, 1986.

Yoder, D. (2003). *Groundhog Day.* Mechanicsburg, PA: Stackpole.

INDEX

Abse, D. W. 90, 102–103, 110
acting out 26
Agdistis 21
Ainslie, R. C. 28, 62
Akhtar, S. 57, 111
Alanen, Y. O. 60
American Psychiatric Association
    48, 116
ancestor's syndrome 29
Apprey, M. 60
Arlow, J. A. 36
Ast, G. xi, 28–29, 37, 41, 60, 62, 91,
    112–114
Atatürk, K. 7
Austen Riggs Center 60

Baatan Death March x
Beres, D. 36
Bergman, A. 33
Bernstein, D. 34
Beutel, M. E. 59

Blackman, J. 33–34
Bloom, P. 53
Blos, P. 15, 62
Blue Ridge Hospital 115–116
Bond, D. D. 107
Bowlby, J. 54
Boyer, L. B. 15, 51, 53, 69–70, 90, 93
brain drain 1
Brazelton, T. B. 53, 60
Brenner, I. 41, 52
Burnham, D. L. 58–60, 110

Cain, A. C. 28, 62
Cain, B. S. 28, 62
Cameron, N. 90–91
Cancro, R. 59
Candlemas Day 12, 17
Castro, F. 102
Cherry Hospital 3, 77
circumcision 45
Comert, P. 37–38, 40